T0146424

ELIXIR:
Women's Quest
FOR *Wholeness*

JESSICA FLEMING

AND

MISHA CROSBIE

BALBOA.
PRESS

A DIVISION OF HAY HOUSE

Balboa Press books may be ordered through booksellers or by contacting:

Balboa Press
A Division of Hay House
1663 Liberty Drive
Bloomington, IN 47403
www.balboapress.com.au
1 (877) 407-4847

Because of the dynamic nature of the Internet, any web addresses or
links contained in this book may have changed since publication and
may no longer be valid. The views expressed in this work are solely those
of the authors and do not necessarily reflect the views of the publisher,
and the publisher hereby disclaims any responsibility for them.

The authors of this book do not dispense medical advice or prescribe
the use of any technique as a form of treatment for physical, emotional,
or medical problems without the advice of a physician, either directly
or indirectly. The intent of the authors is only to offer information
of a general nature to help you in your quest for emotional and
spiritual well-being. In the event you use any of the information in
this book for yourself, which is your constitutional right, the authors
and the publisher assume no responsibility for your actions.

Any people depicted in stock imagery provided by Thinkstock are
models, and such images are being used for illustrative purposes only.
Certain stock imagery © Thinkstock.

Print information available on the last page.

ISBN: 978-1-5043-0511-2 (sc)
ISBN: 978-1-5043-0512-9 (e)

Balboa Press rev. date: 01/04/2017

ELIXIR, by Jessica Fleming and Misha Crosbie, is a book I enthusiastically recommend for all women of heart. Every page pulsates with deep soul wisdom, valuable insights, and loving support for a woman's journey of transformation. If you feel the desire to live fully and express your authentic self with a sense of connectedness, meaning, and purpose, then this book is for you.

The brilliant acronym ELIXIR illuminates each essential step on the path to wholeness, as well as the tools that help you to fulfil that mythic quest.

In reading this concise guide, I am alternately inspired by its powerful truths; tickled by its humour, wordplay, and kiwi turns of phrase; and profoundly moved by its candour and intimacy. With great tenderness and courage, both authors share personal life stories that illustrate each important point and bring it home. These experiences reveal different ways the journey may unfold—how we might hear the inner call for change, refuse to answer the call, and finally set out on the quest to find the ELIXIR, the gift of deeper authenticity and freedom.

On a personal note, I can attest to the integrity, informed wisdom, and dedication to service of these two remarkable women. They are treasured colleagues and friends, and Jessica has been my soul sister for more than three decades.

Their co-creation of this book is a potent distillation of extensive spiritual practice and decades of teaching, sharing, and learning within diverse communities of women and men. The combined experience they express is a gift that I urge you to receive. In addition to the gems they share in this book, if you have the chance to work with Jessica and Misha in person, I wholeheartedly encourage you to seize the opportunity.

—Camille Maurine, author of *Meditation Secrets for Women*

Table of Contents

 **Introduction**

ELIXIR of life—what can it be? Listen,
my friend, and you shall see….. the
Wonder of this Mystery.

What is woman? What is quest? What is wholeness?

Before we begin our chapters of stories that illustrate
particular answers to these big questions, let us explore
the general, archetypal understandings that lie just below
the surface of the waking consciousness in us all. Our
exploration shimmers through our feminine lens of two
women in the new millennium of the 2000s, the signature
of the rise of the feminine—an era of ever-increasing will
to cooperate, mediate, collaborate, and truly listen. This
is the essential energy of two, of twoness, of two together
and working it out.

And this is the hallmark of woman: the capacity to
receive, as with open arms she listens, hears, and receives
the stories, the angst and the joys, and clasps it all to her
heart in the embrace of the circular. The feminine is most
fundamentally expressed in a curved line. As the curve

deepens, it becomes a receptacle, a container. Perhaps the ultimate symbol of this container is the chalice, the precious vessel. Woman/Womb-an as the chalice? Hmm ….

And with what will she choose to fill this precious vessel? Always there is the choice. We have come to Earth school to learn in the University of Free Will. Will you have this or that? Minute by minute, day by day, she listens and chooses. But in the curved cycle of things, there comes a time when she hears a call and knows instinctively that she is to answer the call.

Thus begins the initiatory process called a quest. In fact, all of life can be called a quest. It begins with the going apart from that which came before and the entering into the unknown called life on Earth. We all come with an intention or mission to accomplish in this lifetime. So we begin life sometimes remembering quite a bit but often groping for answers. We gradually find that they come more clearly when we are quiet and alone, when we can look within and deeply listen. The answers also come when we can share our insights and musings and have them deeply honoured and received. Thus, what gradually emerges is the integration, the *aha*s, the gift of remembering who I am and what I am on about in this lifetime. Finally comes the true service, the offering of the gifts and talents in the world—the fulfilling of the mission.

Questing in the ordinary sense is a mini version of the big quest of life. First, there is the vague restlessness, the subtle or more overt signs that something is going to change. Then there is the clarion call that must be answered—the call to go apart into a new territory, the unknown. Seeking, asking, holding an intention. Now the seeker is faced with her fears of possible outer threats, of inner reptiles and dragons. "Can I survive this unknown? This danger? This solitude?" She watches, she waits, she meets the fears, she notices all the signs and synchronicities. She surrenders, she accepts, she finds a pearl of great price. Bit by bit, she integrates—she is seen. Now she is ready for her return to the world. She is bringing her new understanding, the arc of wisdom that she now stands under, to the people and the creatures of this world. She is the same woman who answered the call and went apart. And she is now a new woman, walking her truth with more congruence and grace than ever before.

Questing is an initiatory process and involves leaving something behind for good. It involves stepping across a threshold, a marker, a boundary. It involves irrevocably stepping into the new. It is death and rebirth, not to be undertaken lightly. And yet many of us have heard the call and answered it while not really having a conscious clue.

We simply knew we had to go. This is for the best. If we actually knew what was coming—all the implications, all the changes—we'd be scared to death and would never take the first steps. So we step off the cliff like the Tarot Fool, trusting in a greater something that we will be led, guided, held, supported, and somehow make it through.

What is this greater something? We can call it our spirit. But for women who are relational, who want to relate, perhaps the more accessible something is our soul. This beingness watches over us, nudges through women's gift of intuition, and can be related to as the great friend who is in a state or condition of wholeness. It wants this personality self, this physical body, this emotional expression, this mental acuity to join the soul self fully and in wholeness, together as one. Or in a different vernacular, our souls want our personalities to fully remember that they are whole and live in wholeness. What is wholeness?

The old Middle English word *hal* is the root of three words: whole, health, and holy. By weaving together these three beautiful words, we can begin to feel into the implications. To be whole is to be healthy, which is to be holy. How delightful is that? When I am healthy physically, emotionally, mentally, and spiritually in the whole of my four-body system, then I am in the sacred, I am holy and my whole self.

But what does it mean to be healthy in each quadrant of the four-body system? What does it mean to fully honour the physical temple with nourishing foods and beverages, and with plenty of physical exercise outdoors in the sunlight and fresh air? What does it mean to balance the emotional body with play and laughter, tears of joy and sadness, smiles and frowns, stomping anger and wows of ecstasy? What does it mean to stimulate the mind with healthy inquiry, feeding in heaps of positive and encouraging diet while passing by the dribble of negativity that masquerades as news or gossip? And what does it mean to attend to our spiritual health in prayer and meditation, visualization, and quiet time, in nature or in an enclosed, sacred space?

Living in a state of wholeness is sometimes called the walk in balance. We balance attention and presence with each of our four aspects equally, neglecting none but not overly preoccupied with any one of them. Living in wholeness, healthfulness, and holiness feels like living in heaven on Earth. As the saying goes, "We are the ones we have been waiting for." Perhaps in our ever increasing understanding of the ways of wholeness, we are the harbingers of the present heaven on Earth.

For us, the quest is to fill the chalice with the elixir of wholeness. All of life, every moment, is the quest. Sometimes we are called to go apart for a focused period of questing. In the succeeding chapters, you will explore the quest for the elixir of wholeness with us through its acronym: **E**xit, **L**ook, **I**nside, e**X**amine, **I**ntegrate, **R**eturn. You will read our stories of exciting, challenging circumstances; of being fuelled by knowingness and an intention; of deep inner and outer explorations facing the fears; of examining ourselves, naked in the mirror of truth; of the healing process of witnessing and being witnessed to, gently integrating and finally culminating in our lives' work.

It is our hope and prayer that you will see yourself in some of these stories. We hope they will inspire you to keep on keeping on when the going gets tough. We hope they light you with determination to fill your woman chalice with the elixir of wholeness.

When you **E**xit the norm and **L**ook **I**nside to e**X**amine
your her-story, you will **I**ntegrate the mystery of
you and **R**eturn with the elixir of wholeness.

—Misha Crosbie and Jessica Fleming
Auckland, New Zealand
October 2016

Chapter 1

Exit the Norm: "Something's Gotta Change!"

The Call

How we love the SQ, better known as the status quo. In truth, there is no such thing. Everything is always changing—this is fact. But we regularly delude ourselves into holding on to the idea that finally, at last, everything has settled down, and everything is going to remain nicely the same as right now forever—or at least for a good, long while. Sometimes it looks that way, for a while.

But the truth is nothing ever stays the same. The nature of our world is motion. All things are in motion all the time in this third-dimensional plane called Earth. Whether or not we resist it, the river of life is flowing along. We can become rocks in the river, waiting for the great storm to send us tumbling along. We can pout and shout, stomp and resist, take to our bed with the fevers. Or we can let go into the flow of the river, either with or without what we deem as vital accoutrements such as the boat, oars, food, extra clothes, and maybe even a mask and snorkel. We can lay back, hands behind our heads, and float along in a big trust mode. Or we can prepare and prepare, gathering all we may ever need, and finally let go.

But sooner or later we will have to let go, because of the nudges. Remember, all is in motion both inside and outside. Sooner or later, even the most solid of rocks is going to hear a whisper or feel a slight push of something coming. If there's no answering response, soon the rock will feel a stronger swirl, a call in the wind, an unmistakable call for movement.

And heaven forbid if there's still no answer, no movement. You know what happens next. Some call it the hit over the head, or the cosmic shove. Whatever you call it, it's generally not too pleasant. It appears to dramatically upset your world. It usually calls for at least some measure of that word we have been taught to demean, even despise: surrender. Of course, surrendering is very close to that old, nasty phrase *give up*. We may even be required to allow the final insult: asking for help.

The call can come in many forms. It generally starts with a niggle, almost like an itch at the barest edge of your awareness. You could so easily miss it or dismiss it because it's so subtle. You automatically want to brush it away, like a leaf that softly brushes your skin. "Did I hear something?" Yes, if you are paying attention or have cultivated a practice of noticing even the slightest hints. But most of us haven't.

Along comes the swirling current of a call, which can sound like the buzzing of a mozzie or a fly. Definitely irritating, but definitely a wake-up call. You have to get up and get moving; you have to do something. But what is it? Swat the critter, get rid of it, and lie back down? Or listen a little harder? "Now that I am up, what is it that's trying to get my attention? What was that dream? What am I missing?"

If you are awake enough to begin asking those questions, you'll probably begin noticing some strange coincidences, some synchronicities, some signs from your inner wise woman, some messages from the universe. "The article I just read in the magazine I happened to pick up while waiting in the office. The clear image of a horse in the clouds as I was taking my walk this afternoon. The butterfly that landed on my shoulder yesterday. The conversation with my neighbour, who mentioned Hawai'i—the third time I heard that word today."

Signs and synchronicities come in many ways and forms, and we get a lot of them every day. Mostly they are pretty obvious, and mostly we choose to pay little or no attention to them at all. We could, though. We could cultivate the habit of noticing and paying attention, learning from and getting the guidance from these signs. Mostly we don't, which is too bad because the consequences then become not fun.

We have all had a sledgehammer treatment or known someone who has. It often looks like a challenging health situation, a devastating loss of some kind, or an accident that changes everything. Whatever the event or process, it's as though you have been stripped bare, taken down to the bones, and left to stew. It asks you to listen deeper than ever before; really hear the call for change. It's a call you will never forget. Bit by bit, slowly and gradually in the enforced surrendering and deeper listening, you can come to an acceptance of the call, of the changes, of the wisdom that is growing in you.

Maybe you've heard the whisper and paid attention. Maybe you've read the message of the horse in the cloud. Maybe you've had the horrendous car accident, disease, divorce, or death of a loved one, and you've been forced to surrender to the quiet listening. Whatever your way—and they're all good in the big picture—the call will come. What was will pass away, will Exit.

Before you stretches the unknown, and it's very scary. You can try to run or hide, but the movement is inexorable. There has been a little death, and you are required to face it. By facing it, you begin to see intimations of the new. With every death, every ending, there is always a new beginning. The **E**xit is the entrance, the revolving door in the dance of life. May we all **E**xit as gracefully as possible when the call comes.

Misha's Story

At age fifteen, I attended a vocations camp at Knockna Gree, ostensibly to accompany my girlfriend who seriously wanted to be a nun. I hadn't been away from home to a camp or any holiday in my teenage years, so this sounded like a great opportunity. I convinced myself that I didn't really have to consider a religious vocation in order to go to the camp. My goal was to get married and have a family of ten kids: two sets of twins, one set of triplets, and the other three any way they came. But to qualify for the camp, I had to have the recommendation of our school. That was easy; all I had to say was that I would like to go to the camp, and there were no further questions asked. There were four of us from our fifth form class (year eleven) who eventually attended.

In terms of a vocation in life, I wanted to be a doctor but was told that nursing was what was open to girls. This was the early sixties, an era when nursing, teaching, or being a secretary were the usual choices open to women. If you were a Catholic, you could give your life to God in service as a nun. Nowadays there are so many more options for service at home and abroad.

For the most part, I had been schooled through the Catholic system, and in my impressionable years and beyond, we were told and read the stories of the saints, men, and women who gave their lives in service to God. The majority ended their lives in martyrdom and stayed faithful to their beliefs and service in spite of the brutality of the martyrdom. I hid a guilty secret from age twelve, when in class we were asked, after the completion of the story of Saint Maria Goretti (she was murdered at that age for protecting her virginity), if we were prepared to die for our faith. I put my hand up along with the rest of the class, but in my heart of hearts, I was scared of pain and torture and knew that I could easily betray my faith if the pain was too great. I was a post-war child and had a steady diet of war films in which torture was a key feature. I shuddered to think of having my nails torn off, being burnt, or whatever cruelty a human could concoct. I wanted to believe the affirmative that I had just given, but my guilty secret was that I feared I would be a coward in the face of such a choice.

In actuality, I already knew I was a coward because I had been sexually molested in boarding school by one of the older girls and by the parish priest—and in form one, by a family acquaintance. I knew I hadn't fought to the death to stop their actions, so it was a no-brainer that I would choose marriage rather than religious life. And yet even as a small child, I was drawn to service. I had expressed a desire to go to Mars to be a missionary, because some of the radio stories that I'd listened to at my Nana's on a Friday night about Martians captured my imagination. In flights of fancy, I could see myself going to unchartered territory and winning souls for God.

The paradox of the vocations camp experience is that towards the end of the week, I felt the call to religious service as genuinely as was possible for a fifteen-year-old. I was shocked because it was not why I had gone; this camp was meant to be a holiday with my best friend. I kept this experience to myself and tried to push it away. How could a girl who was afraid of being a coward, to the point of denying God if she were tortured, consider having a vocation? But one doesn't *have* a vocation—one is *called*. And once the call is received, it is compelling. I know I didn't hear a voice calling me, and I equally know

I wasn't pressured by the two people running the camp. But what I heard about a religious life of service struck a chord in me. I just knew. I didn't have words to describe that knowing, but I had family members, especially my Nana and my parents, who raised me to be of service to others. I had been in Catholic boarding school from the ages of five to ten, so I was familiar with convent life; it seemed to be a natural progression. And in the early sixties, there were limited opportunities for serving God.

Once back from camp, I flowed back into my daily life, the call receded into the back of my consciousness, and I never spoke of it. I was a typical Catholic teenager of the time and was involved in school and parish activities, particularly the youth club of our parish. We played sport, we had socials, and I was active in youth leadership.

The following year, my sixth form year (year twelve), we were called individually by the principal to discuss our future aspirations. I was one of the first to go to interview, so there was no time to prepare—remember the teaching, nursing, and secretary options! When asked what I was thinking of, I said calmly and clearly that I felt called to enter religious life. I was more shocked than she was to hear myself enunciate those words, and yet it was my truth. I learned then I would be trained for teaching. That was difficult because I had set my heart on nursing once I'd learned that I wasn't able to be a doctor. I had read every novel about nursing, had read June Opie's story five or six times, and had spent times in my holidays going to help at the surgery where our good family friend was the nurse. At least I wasn't going to be tortured!

I completed my school year, and in February the following year, instead of returning for form 6a (year thirteen), I **E**xited my home and entered religious life. There was no turning back from the call—it was impelling and compelling, and once I had named the call, I had no hesitation in answering. For my parents, as Catholics this was a supreme moment: one of their children had heard and answered the call. It was only after my first nine months in the order—my postulancy, a time of preparation to see if the order was prepared to accept me into the novitiate—that I learned from a letter my mother wrote to me how the call and my exiting their home had been for her. She wrote, "As a Catholic, I feel very proud; as a mother, all I feel is an empty space."

Jessica's Story

How could anything go wrong with the "perfect marriage"? I had had a first marriage that brought in my two beautiful children, but Mose and I were as unsuited as corn and hibiscus. I had consulted an outstanding channel, Dr. Neva Dell Hunter, who had assured me that if I completed the karma with him by biting my tongue and being as patient and kind as possible (a very tough ask for a young Aries), he would eventually leave. Then another man would show up who was older, wiser, wealthy, and on the same spiritual wavelength. I did, and he did.

Dean and I had a glorious time travelling in Europe and America, attending all kinds of New Age trainings and seminars, and offering some ourselves. We established a New Age retreat and workshop centre in Albuquerque and sponsored programs by some of the outstanding leaders of the day, including Peter and Eileen Caddy of Findhorn fame and Dr. Helen Bonny of the Bonny Method of Guided Imagery and Music. I was training in this outstanding counselling modality as a postgraduate supplement to my master's degree in mental health counselling. We were happily doing our work and fulfilling our lifetime missions—weren't we? The outstanding astrologer we had consulted gave us the best possible date and time for our wedding, and we adhered to it exactly. We believed that we would walk into the sunset of our lives, serving the Great Plan together.

About five years after our marriage in 1974, I had a nudge of attraction to another man. This hadn't happened before, and I was surprised. But it was no big deal, right? The very next year, Dean and I were in a blinding snowstorm car crash. We both had concussions, but Dean almost died. As we lay recuperating in the hospital, we tried to discern the message. My answer was: simplify!

Our lives had become so busy and overcommitted that we were both exhausted. Dean had extended our portfolio to include one more property. Altogether the stress was over the top. We came back to our beautiful, peaceful centre overlooking the Rio Grande and the Sandia Mountains. I was lolling in the upper room, mostly in la-la land. It was beyond shocking when Dean announced a short time later that he had bought yet another big property. In retrospect, I know that something in me snapped.

We continued along quite nicely until one fine day Dean told me he was having an affair. It transpired that he was desperate to talk with someone who had also had a near-death experience (NDE), about which I had wanted to hear nothing. He was grieving the loss of the "other side's" magnificence, but I wanted him here and now, simplifying. Therefore he found an NDE lady he could talk with, and he began encouraging me towards an open marriage. He assured me his affair did not in any way threaten our marriage.

After many months of this dialogue, I sat up all night reading the book called *Open Marriage*. Towards dawn I resolved that I would also open myself to whatever was in divine order, including another relationship. That afternoon, Dean came home and announced his affair had ended. Sadly, I related that I had opened another door. We could now both see the handwriting on the wall.

It was no surprise when a casual friend of Dean's knocked on the door several months later. The instant and powerful attraction between me and this handsome stranger was acknowledged on all sides. Richard and I began some fabulous and exotic travelling, including New Zealand and Australia where we swam with some free dolphins at Monkey Mia, north of Perth.

But I also began a deep inquiry myself. I attended my first vision quest under the expert tutelage of Michael Brown, and I discovered the hidden anger I had toward my "perfect" mentor and husband. I saw how my good-girl upbringing had conditioned me to follow in the footsteps of others, but whom? The husband—especially the good, kind, wise, spiritual husband. It had been unthinkable to question the "perfect" husband.

I looked deeply into the teaching about cycles. As the excellent adage goes, "Some things [people] are in your life for a reason, some for a season, some for a lifetime." I looked back with heartbreak on our beautiful life together, our beautiful centre, and our beautiful dreams. Somehow, little by little I accepted that the marriage was over, that the life we had together was over. It was truly Exit time.

Then I had the dream. There was a huge fire, and our centre was burning down. I was desperate to get inside and retrieve some of the precious things, but I could only reach my hand around the door and close my fist around a bundle of jewels before I had to leave.

I called the dream "Take the gems and go." It signalled that completion was nigh: I had what I needed (the gems), and it was time to move along, though I knew not where.

In New Zealand, people had repeatedly said to me, "And when you move here …" They paid little attention when I assured them I was happy in America and would not be moving to New Zealand (where I have now lived for twenty-seven years). Yes, there were fine clues about the doors that were to open, but I dismissed them at the time as untenable, unthinkable. I was an American, and that was that!

My, my, how we can dig in and resist. I hope you have never been so stubborn. But most likely you've at least had some of those tendencies. Most of us do. Therefore I have created an **E**xit mantra that sometimes helps: "Let go sooner!"

May it help you too.

Chapter 2

Look: "Why Am I Doing This?"

The Intention

The call has come, whether in a lullaby or a gale. It is unmistakable and unavoidable. Naturally, there are two voices in your head, perhaps politely discussing the options or vehemently vying for your attention. One says, "Why in the world would I upset the status quo and change my comfortable (but increasingly uncomfortable) situation?" The other voice says, "We've gotta go, baby. We're done here."

Somewhere in the midst, we notice a rational voice saying, "Calm down, sister. Let's have a Look!" We check out the pros and cons, and we even make lists. We feel into the old and the possible new. We can't avoid the fidgety discomforts of the old, though we try to. Contemplation of the unknown ranges from mildly exciting to outright terrifying.

We talk to people—oh, do we talk. Siblings, parents, relatives of all sorts, neighbours, fellow team members, friends, classmates, teachers, grocery store checkout people, even counsellors. Sometimes we even listen to them in return. We take courses, go to trainings, and sit through lectures by people who "have the answers." Mostly we gather data and opinions, sifting and sorting and weighing and brewing.

For some, the Look is all interior: endless explorations of the what-ifs, the maybes, or the how-tos. A lot of mental "Ring around the Rosie." Sometimes it's transferred into highly useful writing; it could be one's own journal pages, or pages of stream of consciousness that yield astounding titbits of crystal clarity. It could be emails that may or may not be sent, or a Word document that may or may not be printed. It could even be Facebook postings, but we hope not. Please limit those to closed, trustworthy groups.

For others, the interior look has the quality of prayer or dialogue with your version of the Greater Than. It could be a god or goddess, or your higher self, or your guardian angel, or Jesus or Buddha, or your medicine animal, or whomever. However you choose to name the Greater Than is not the issue. That there is a Greater Than can be a clarity of enormous assistance in accepting the Exiting process.

There are a few blessed folks amongst us who get the call and have the instant knowing and acceptance that this is what is next—the blinding flash of the obvious, or BFO (thank you, Trish). The Look for these people really has more to do with gratitude and preparation for implementing the intention to Exit. One could say they have received an intuitive download that immediately feels right to them, or one could say that they have a highly developed faith in divine guidance. Whatever you call it, these instances, like Misha's story in chapter one, are marked by a graceful simplicity. There is no angst. There is no prolonged decision-making process, no back-and-forthness. Just get on with it. There's okayness and on-track-ness.

Whether your Look in response to the Exit call seems more like Jessica's lengthy reflective process or Misha's BFO, there are intrinsic qualities or components in the Look: the mobilizing of will and courage that develops self confidence, the accessing of knowledge that becomes wisdom, the opening to insights that transform into understanding, the growth in flexibility that leads to growth in consciousness.

It takes great courage and fortitude to stare the little death, the big change in the face. Often you have to pull up resources from way down deep in order to even

Look at the Exit call. The contemplation of what will be required to complete the exit, never mind the actions themselves, necessarily catalyze and strengthen your personal will, your can-do spirit, your solar plexus chakra of empowerment. Congratulate yourself now if you have ever stared down a big change. You are stronger for it, and you deserve to let your self-esteem shine.

You are wiser for it too. All that data you accumulated to make or action the Exit strategies, to catalyze your intention; all that knowledge concerning options, the possibilities that lay before you; all that discernment of which way, this way, the other way—they coalesced into a wiser you! It turns out wisdom is a rare commodity in these days of instant everything. Congratulate yourself again for the wisdom shining through you.

Then there is the understanding that gradually dawns through the accretion of all those insights, those mini BFOs through the Looking. It is said that the feet represent the place of understanding in our bodies, standing under the rest of the body and carrying us through the walks of life, including the big change walks. We like to think that all the insights gained from the Look travelled from our brain right down to our tippy toes, based there as ever increasing understanding. Congratulations again for the past, present, or even future Look that has added to your understanding.

And who can be present with big change, with Exit possibilities, without the dance of flexibility? Even if you're a rock, the tumble tongs will grab hold of you. As we all know and feel, these are big change times in the collective. Before we even deal to the personal, they are calling us to ever-increasing flexibility. Add a big change, an Exit call in your own life, and wow! Even the Looking, the contemplating, the reflecting takes you into a super waltz.

But wait—there's rhyme and reason in all this upheaval. Because what's our species-wide human mission on this beloved blue green gem of a planet called Earth? To raise consciousness. Yes, the wise kids of the 1960s had a handle on it, called consciousness raising. That's what each and every one of us is here for.

Every time you have the courage to Look an Exit call in the face, gathering knowledge, insights, and flexibility to formulate your intention(s) for the Exit, you are beautifully contributing to our collective mission. You are growing yourself and growing us in consciousness. A final congratulation for every contribution you have ever made or will make.

See you in the Looking mirror!

Misha's Story

My mother was a tall, auburn-haired Leo who had a great energy and passion for life. One couldn't help but notice her presence wherever she went as she exuded confidence (not always felt by her, I might add) and common sense born of the life journey she had been on. As a child, her passion and prowess was sport; school was a necessary thing to do, but it gave her lots of opportunities for team sports. I was a dreamier, bookish child who had an idea a minute but would get around to them someday, whereas she believed, "If you think it, then do it. Make it happen." As I was growing up with her during my intermediate and high school years, she had a couple of sayings that stuck in my memory. The first one was, "Up here for thinking [pointing to her head] and down here for dancing [pointing to her feet]." I heard this saying over and over again because I would make three or four trips to accomplish what she would do in one. For example, I was single-minded and would go to the kitchen to set the table, whereas she would pick up the laundry and put it in the wash house on her way to the kitchen. I am not sure that I have really learned that lesson, because I still hear her voice as I do one thing at a time. Yes, I can multitask today, but I could be more efficient!

Her other saying that has stayed with me over the years and become part of my philosophy is, "If there is a job to be done [in the community], join the committee and get on with it. If there is no committee, start one, and you might as well be the president." My mother was open to change, and when she saw the need for it, she would work toward making that change happen. Sometimes her readiness for change was challenging for those around her who were not so proactive and were comfortable with the way things were, or at least with the current pace of change. She was diplomatic and understanding, but she would still venture forward, inviting those around her to join her in the action. She was very popular in her circle in the parish and amongst her friends, who recognized her leadership and enthusiasm, but she had her detractors as well. She taught me to "see the more and not settle for less."

And so I entered the order, trained as a teacher, and embarked on a wonderfully satisfying and fulfilling life of teaching, first with primary schoolchildren, then intermediate, and finally secondary. I loved being with the youngsters, and at my first school in Rotorua, I would play four-square with them at playtime, join in with the softball games, and have lunchtime coaching for basketball. I was twenty-two at the time and was much younger than the parents of the forty-five youngsters I taught. I could express my exuberance for life with them, and I missed them when they were on school holidays and I was with the grown-ups at the convent! At my next school in Auckland, I had more responsibilities, so I wasn't able to (or encouraged to) play with the youngsters, but I loved teaching them. Life in the order had its niggles, which I did my best to overlook, reminding myself that none of us is perfect.

But I was starting to feel somewhat stifled in the convent environment. There were little things that seemed unkind, and I had a growing awareness that there were other things we could be doing in the parish rather than weeding our rose garden. It was there that I first allowed myself to think there has to be something more to life. And there was a pivotal moment that turned that niggle into a festering sore.

One evening just after dinner, there was a banging at our front door, and a very distressed woman asked to come in for shelter because she was sure her husband was trying to murder her. Yes, she was under the doctor, and when we spoke to him, he said that she was unwell and was safe with him. I was instructed to take her home after one of the others had rung the husband. Much against my better judgement and after much arguing with the sister in charge, I drove her home. Was she unwell, or did she have good reason to be scared? Even if she was mentally unwell, her fear was real. Several of us wanted to give her a bed for the night so that the situation could be dealt with in the light of day. The husband would know she was safe with us, and she could calm down and feel safer. But it was not to be. All the way to her house, she begged me not to take her to her husband. I dropped her off feeling like a betrayer. I was obedient because I was afraid of the repercussions if I didn't do as I was told. I had shades of the young girl I had been, frightened that she was a coward.

I came back to our convent angry and confused, and I went into the chapel because I had missed night prayers with the others. I took out my office book but couldn't face saying the prayers after turning away a woman in need. I flung the office book across the room and screamed, "What am I doing? What are we about? Dear God, surely this isn't right!" What was left of my rose-tinted glasses shattered in that instant. They fell away completely when I ran into this woman several days later, and she hissed at me, "I am safe—but no thanks to you."

Life changed for me then, and I began questioning blind obedience and doing things "just because." I moved schools and community and began teaching at a secondary school. This was a completely different experience from the homeliness and familiarity of primary and intermediate, where one had one's own class. I adapted and embarked on seven years of teaching at this level, but the door had been opened to my questioning, and I could not reconcile some of the teachings of the Church and the lives of the young women in front of me. Again I faced the feeling that there had to be something more.

During this time, in 1979 my beloved Nana died in the January. She had been a point of stability and unconditional love (as grandmothers often are) in a somewhat troubled childhood. With her passing, the ground on which I stood became precarious. This was reflected in a repeating dream I had from childhood. I was standing on the wooden platform of the stairs on the outside of a building, with a pirate underneath slashing away at the platform. This dream returned when Nana died. By May of that year, I was seriously ill with glandular fever and associated complications, and I was in hospital from mid-May till early July. Nobody, least of all myself, recognized the depth of my grieving. With hindsight, I can see that the niggles of something more were compounded by the inner grieving for Nana. After all, it wasn't my mother who had died—it was "just" my grandmother, as people said.

In 1980 I was surer that I needed to seek the "something more," and I expressed a desire to leave the order. I was assured it was a professional unease rather than a crisis of vocation. It was decided that I was to go to a personal and spiritual development course of renewal in Melbourne so that I could get my bearings. At the end of that first year, I had a repeat of my earlier dream, except that the platform on which I stood was metal with no threatening presence beneath it. Finally, I was on solid ground once more. The following year, I studied theology and spiritual direction at Yarra Theological Union, but an old, persistent condition resulted in my having a hysterectomy. I might have been standing on firmer ground, but that surgery was a sign that all was not well in my world.

I came back to Auckland at the end of the two years and trained as a counsellor. This led me into working while within the order with diverse populations: pregnant teenagers at Bethany, women and men addicted to heroin at Higher Ground, and out-of-control teenage boys at Youthlink. Yes, I had been supported to change my profession from teaching to counselling, but there was still that voice calling me, insisting there was something more. I loved my work but wasn't happy in the confines of the order. My soul wasn't being fed by the religious practices we followed, and I felt parched and dry. Try as

I might to convince myself otherwise—after all, I had made life vows—I could not shake off the feeling that I might be being called to leave this place of security and familiarity.

Around this time, I had a very telling dream. I was standing outside of a field that was barren and dry. In it, there were hundreds of crows bent over and pecking at the dry soil, trying to find sustenance. This dream led to much soul searching. What were those crows mirroring to me? Was I one of them pecking at arid ground, trying to find my spiritual sustenance? Was this what I had become? How did this happen? What happened to the exuberant fifteen-year-old who had clearly heard the call some twenty-six years ago? Was this the so-called dark night of the soul that I had read about? I had weathered other dark nights in earlier years, but this seemed as if every light had been extinguished. Was I really just pecking in vain at the arid soil of my soul? Was this all that was ahead of me? Surely there had to be something more. I wrestled inwardly in this darkness. On the outside, I was fulfilling my mission and seemingly happy, but inwardly I was beyond confused.

Dare I look that dream image in the face and see the signs, or did I stay true to my vows? Poverty and chastity were not threatened, but my vow of obedience was. For twenty-five years I had been a good sister and had worked faithfully and obediently to the voice of God, spoken to me through the voices of the sisters in charge. I thought back to the voice that had instructed me to take that fearful, suffering woman home, as well as other incidents. My health had taken quite a battering over those years. And yet …

I agonized over obedience. Whose voice was I hearing? The voice of God enunciated by the pope, the bishops, and the sisters in charge? They were the authorities. Often what I heard them say was in direct contradiction to what we espoused in our mission. What about the still, small voice within when I sat in meditation? I read somewhere at the time that the root meaning of the word *authority* was about "making to grow." But I wasn't growing. I was standing in an arid field, pecking nonsensically, and hoping to find sustenance. I had to keep looking within and not distract myself from the truth by getting more and more involved with my outer work. Back in Melbourne some years before, I'd stood up in class one day and in great pain announced that I didn't know who God was anymore; moreover, I didn't think I believed in one. The room emptied quickly, and one of the spiritual directors was called. She listened carefully to my incoherent ramblings and advised me to simply stop praying and going to rituals. I should rest and listen until I found my way again in whatever form that revealed itself. Whose voice had I been listening to?

What transpired is that the voice I heard calling me all those years ago at Knockna Gree seemed to be saying I could no longer live the call in my current environment. I was no longer growing spiritually through the avenues that were offered to me in the order. After this extended Look within I left the order in 1989, taking with me the advice of the sister in charge at the time. She said to me as she accepted my resignation, "Go out and live your calling in the wider world." My intention was formulated.

Jessica's Story

The handsome stranger, Richard, had appeared, and off we went exploring to the ends of the earth, or at least the other side of the planet.

Synchronistically, I had met Bruce, who was effusive on the subject of cetacean research. Who are the dolphins and whales, really, given their brains are much bigger than ours? Bruce said, "And when you go to New Zealand and Australia …"

I replied, "Where are they? I am not going there!"

At the time, I was training in the counselling modality, the Bonny Method of Music and Imagery. There was surprise but no shock when I received a call for presentations at the First International Imagery Conference. Where? Queenstown, New Zealand. I sent a proposal that was accepted, and we were off—six and a half months tootling around New Zealand and Australia, even swimming with the wild dolphins at Monkey Mia, north of Perth. It was a blissful, harmonious journey during which people in New Zealand kept saying, "And when you move here …" I kept answering, "I love your country, and it is fantastically beautiful, but I'm *not* moving here!"

Richard and I settled back into life in America, and once again I was in the "perfect relationship." Wasn't I? My dear friend and mentor, Beth Gawain (the wise mother of Shakti Gawain), got in my face and said, "Jessica, it is *not* perfect." She and I had met in a hot tub in New Zealand, and it was she who had taken us to Monkey Mia, introducing us to her dolphin friends Nicky and Holey Fin. We three had travelled to Yosemite, California, and into the Banana Clan Kiva in New Mexico. She saw, and she knew what I didn't and couldn't see.

Richard began having an affair with a younger woman. My heart was broken, but I told myself that he'd get over it. My lovely New Zealand friend, Erica Light, wrote regularly and asked me to come visit. I did, and I loved it. I counselled quite a few people, made a lot of connections, and wondered. On my return, Richard was as wonderful as ever to me, but he was still seeing the other woman. I ranted and raved, begged and pleaded, saw psychics, talked it all over with everyone, and went back to New Zealand the next year. More openings, more professional acclaim, more acceptance.

I was back home with Richard one more time, and I was really Looking. Could I truly make a life for myself in New Zealand? Could I be on my own without a man at my side for the first time in my life? Could I actually provide for myself and look after myself? Like many women, I come from a long lineage of women who were not able to contemplate life without a husband. The men had the power, the money, and the mana. My mother had divorced her alcoholic husband, and it had nearly killed her. But Beth Gawain was divorced and had provided for herself very nicely, thank you very much. She'd travelled the world for fourteen years living a fabulously exotic life. Could I?

The Look went on and on with pros and cons. Could I, dared I? What if? The doors were opening in New Zealand and closing in the States. What about my children? They were getting along nicely with their lives. What about my siblings and all the people I looked after in the States? They'd survive. Some may even thrive without me. How could that be? And what about me? Would I survive?

The internal debates raged deep into the nights. When a colleague from New Zealand suggested, "Let's set up a counselling centre," I felt the final piece clunk into place. It was a vision, a focus, an intention, a purpose that could move me forward. I knew how to set up a centre; hadn't I participated in doing just that in New Mexico? I knew how to counsel; hadn't I been doing that all my life? I had a lot of new friends and some clients waiting for me in New Zealand. I could move, and I would. My few possessions went into storage, and I sold the beautiful Audi that Richard had bought for me.

With a trembling heart, away I went to a brave new world, feeling utterly welcomed there and yet a stranger in a new land. The Look had served me well enough that I found the courage, created the intention, and developed the faith that somehow, someway it would work out.

And so it was. And so it has. Blessed be.

Chapter 3

Inside: "Yikes!"

The Solitude

In life overall, and in a formalized quest, there comes a time for the solo—a time apart, time on your own. As with any big adventure, this is both exciting and scary, even terrifying. No matter how much you have prepared, when the time comes, you are alone in unfamiliar circumstances, and it is up to you to handle it.

Well, not quite. In truth, you always have help. In a formalized quest, there is always at least one guide (usually several) holding the energy for you as you go forth to face the dragons. The guide remains at whatever base camp has been established and holds a vision of your safety, as well as the fulfilment of your intention for the quest. The guide is your anchor keeping vigil for you, like a safety net. Yes, the guide may be some distance from your solo area, but he or she is there nonetheless, both psychically and physically.

Ah, the comfort of knowing that you are being energetically held, and knowing that you will return eventually and be welcomed in the knowledge that your stories, your intuitions, and your clarities will be heard and respected. All these knowings support a freedom in your exploring—a freedom to follow your inner nudges, go where you choose, and do what you will. Most important, freedom to let it happen. Let go, listen to your belly wisdom, and allow.

This is a time to cultivate a quiet alertness, an open awareness, a readiness Inside for whatever. A _ of somethings will occur, and your job is to notice everything. Notice what's happening in your body. Notice how the breeze is caressing your arms, or how the winds whip around your head. Notice what's flying through the sky or crawling on the ground. Notice the incredible colours and shapes around you. Notice what pictures or images are arising in your mind. Notice everything!

Most important, notice what fears are arising Inside: fear of the dark, fear of animals, fear of enclosed spaces, fear of the expanse, fear of the weather, fear of your own mind going wild with its ghosts and demons, fear that you have carried since childhood, imaginary fears, realistic fears. This is the time to face these fears. Look them in the eye and be present with them, and lo and behold, watch them dissolve in to the vapours that they are.

In your openness and heightened expectancy, you are also anticipating gifts, treasures, and most likely at least one pearl of great price. It will often be presented when you least expect it. Maybe you will have a dream. Maybe it will be clear as day, or maybe you will have to wait for your guides to help you interpret it. Or maybe you will have a vision, a new name, an encounter with an animal, or a message from the stars or clouds. Whatever it is, treasure it and hold it close as you gratefully bring your solo to completion.

And what if it is a life solo, and there are no human guides to support you and help you through a big transition? What if you are truly on your own physically, knowing that what you come back to will never be the same? Perhaps you may never come back to where you were. These life solos—times of enormous change, leaving behind, moving in to the unknown—are the biggest challenges. Any health crisis, separation or death, moving far away, or radical change in circumstances offers a life solo. Yes, there may be people you can turn to for solace, both familiar faces and people from out of the blue. But truly this is your time to reach deep Inside. Reach like you have never reached before. Reach for the courage that lies in your good, steady bones. Reach for the strength that flows through your good, red blood. And reach beyond your little self to the Greater Than in whatever form attracts you.

Because there *is* a Greater Than—something greater than your personal self, something that organizes the universe, something greater that you are a part of, something that actually cares about you and has your highest good in mind. It doesn't matter what you call that something. Feel free to call it what you will, but call it. It is there for you and has your back. And it can help you more fully when you ask for help. Ask for guidance, and ask to be shown the way. That is a law or universal principle: spirit is around and through you all the time, but it cannot interfere or assist you in specific ways unless you ask. Trust and ask for help. Ask more, and you will find that more will be given. You will come home to yourself in deeper and fuller ways.

You will come to know yourself Inside in ways you never dreamed possible. You will build communion with your soul and find that it is your best friend, your truest ally that is always there for you. You will come to love your practice of turning within, in your form of prayer or meditation. You will feel that solace from within, the gentlest yet strongest reassurance and holding that you have ever felt.

Thus the solo, the look **I**nside, becomes one of the most important and valuable things you have ever done. Whether you actively choose it by joining an arranged quest, or set up your own circumstances with a trusted guide, or find the solo time thrust upon you by life circumstances, do your best to embrace it despite your trembling. You will be gifted beyond measure, and you will know yourself **I**nside in deeper and richer ways than ever before.

Misha's Story

At age forty-two, as I left my religious order, I faced a world of which I had limited knowledge in the sense of making a living, providing my own housing, and living without community. After all, I had lived in a community since the age of five in my first boarding school. I did have six years from ages eleven to sixteen living within my family, and they were wonderful years. Our stepfather embraced my brother and me when he fell in love with our mother and married her in 1956. My brother and I returned home to live with them in 1957. Our dad, along with Mum, made sure that to the best of their ability, we had all the necessities of life. They both worked to give us a stable home and a good Catholic education, but in the early days there was often more week than wages. They taught us to live simply and value what we had, and to not pine after that which we couldn't afford. One of Dad's big lessons was, "Don't buy anything you cannot afford. Save up, and when you have the resources, then go buy what you need." During high school, my brother and I worked during the holidays, he in the wool sheds and I in the local laundry, to help our parents cover the costs of our school fees. We learned that we worked hard for what we had, and if necessary, we worked more than one job to make ends meet.

In the order, I did not have to manage money—everything was provided. I always had enough food, clothing, and housing, and a ten-day holiday was provided at our beach house each year. All my basic needs were met, and I was also given the opportunities to gain my teaching certificate and my undergraduate degree. The work ethic I had learned at home was reinforced, and I was never one to shirk hard work.

In October 1989, I found myself in charge of myself and all of my needs. I joined forces with a woman friend who was leaving her order at the same time, and with the money we both had received on leaving, we were able to put down a modest deposit on a house. In reality, we were the proud owners of the front door, because we had a major mortgage. She had more smarts than I did about money because she had been running a boarding school. In the order, all the wages we earned in our respective jobs went into the central fund. Now I was receiving a fortnightly pay with money left over after I had paid my share of the expenses. For a few months, I gave away that money because I had no need of it. I soon learned that I needed to save, but at first I was uncomfortable with having what I saw as surplus. I continued in the work I was doing at Youthlink when I left the order, so I knew myself in that capacity.

But what about the core of me? I no longer had to be obedient to a superior; there were no rules other than the rules of society. Who was I really? On one hand, nothing was different: I got up and went to work, I ate, and I socialized. But on the other hand, everything was different: I was solely responsible for me, and I was living out my mission of mercy. I was solely responsible for providing for my needs. At forty-two, could I make my way in the world when I was ignorant about much of it? I had a simplicity and a naiveté, but I was also educated and had been in the workforce, so I knew I could make my way there.

But my soul needed feeding, and I had no idea how to go about that. I latched onto the advice I had been given seven years earlier in Melbourne: stop praying and going to rituals. So it was that I left the order *and* left the practices of the Catholic Church. As the saying goes, I went from hero to zero overnight. Various members of my family came to grips with my being released from those solemn life vows I had taken in St. Patrick's Cathedral all those years ago and not remaining a practicing Catholic, which in the vernacular of the day was termed a lapsed Catholic. Years later, when I was finally able to confront the sexual abuse at age nine at the hands of the parish priest where I was in boarding school, I came to the realization that I was not a lapsed Catholic but a collapsed Catholic. What the confessional priest did by authoritatively scolding me for being the wrong and sinful one set up within me a crisis of faith that was to take years to heal. In my day, the priest was feted as the voice of God for the rest of us Catholics. As schoolchildren, he was God, so to speak. In my shame and guilt that I could be so bad, I tried desperately to be a good Catholic girl so that I could gain forgiveness for the terrible deeds I had done. "God" had spoken and pronounced me bad to my core.

A couple of years before I left the order, a small group of us had gone on our annual ten-day retreat, which that year was held at our beach house on Waiheke Island. Each day was alone time, except for attending mass in the morning and a one-hour spiritual direction session every second day. I sat on the clifftop and incessantly gazed at the incoming and outgoing tide on Oneroa Beach. I was confused and frightened. My aloneness was empty—there was nothing I could relate to, my prayers were wooden and directed to a God who confused me.

Two incidents happened on the same day some hours apart. A young man came with his dog to the beach, and he wanted the dog to play in the waves with him. He would call out, and the dog would come to the edge of the water and hang back. No matter how much the young man called to him, the dog didn't come into the water. Finally, the young man lost patience and pulled the dog by the collar, dragging him into the water with the dog yelping and resisting. When the dog was over his depth, the man let him go, and the dog frantically swam to shore and lay down on the sand. The young man got out soon after and walked past the dog without acknowledging him. The dog followed with his tail between his legs. I was so angry at what I had witnessed that I broke down in inconsolable sobbing. That was undoubtedly the loneliest moment in my life, a moment of truth that like that dog, I was a total failure. I had been called, but I was too much of a coward to plunge into the deep, and I too was being ignored and punished. I continued to stare at the waves breaking on the sand until I was numb with grief.

Several hours later, another young man came with his dog, and I panicked that the same thing was going to happen. I determined that if it did, I would go down to the beach and intervene. Happily, the young man had the patience to coax his dog gently and with support, lying in the shallow water and calling him, talking to him, and encouraging him. Eventually the two of them were out in the water, with the young man right there with his dog. As they left from their swim, the young man was patting the dog and talking to him. I couldn't make out the words, but the dog responded with a wagging tail. For me these two happenings were mirrors of my relationship with God. The angry, demanding punishing God because I didn't measure up and was such a coward and a sookie. The other was the loving father who called and encouraged and supported until I could brave the waves and swim on my own. This split between being loved and rejected because I was bad dogged me for many years to come.

Although my friend and I lived together in our house, I was truly alone for the first time in my life. I had known loneliness, especially in boarding school and in community, but I had not truly been alone. This was a new dimension for me. I needed to Look inside myself and see whether anyone of consequence was there. Without my religious practices to cover me, I came up short when I looked Inside. When I sat down to meditate or pray, I didn't know to whom to pray. My friend was on her own journey and seemed to find comfort in some Buddhist practices, but I didn't relate to practices of any sort. There was this relational emptiness inside as I sat in my aloneness, so I filled that space with work and rebuilt my outer self, who was smarting from the fall from hero to zero.

In 1991 two defining events happened. First, I signed up for a counselling training course in a modality called the Bonny Method of Music and Imagery. My friend and I had both embarked on our masters degree in counselling, and this particular modality was being offered as an extra. I didn't really have much exposure to classical music, but I was drawn to try it out. A small group of us attended six weekly evening sessions. Finally, in the lying down and being led into the music, my soul responded and was touched in every nook and cranny. I was held and supported by the music and challenged by the music, but I never felt abandoned. I felt the imagery journey rather than saw it, and I gradually overcame my fear of drawing when we were invited to express our journeys through drawing mandalas. At last, my soul self was having an expression and being mirrored back to me through the mandalas. Here was a way to be alone and dive deep to touch my soul.

If the first event had my soul opening, the second event brought me to my knees. My mother was diagnosed with cancer in December 1991, and we were told it would be a journey of months, not years. I had been on that journey with a friend in Australia in 1990, supporting her through her final days with cancer, so I knew what to do. However, this was my mother, only sixty-six years of age, and it seemed that my newfound relationship with soul was being challenged. How could he do this to her? She was a good Catholic woman who did the very best she knew how in life. She was a leader and a shaker and a mover, and she was much loved in her outdoor bowling community. My heart was pained as I supported my parents through their final months together—a journey to which our father gave himself wholeheartedly in order to make every moment Mum had as loving and as supported as possible. Mum died in August 1992 just one week shy of her sixty-seventh birthday.

Early in 1992, I went deeper into the Bonny Method of Music and Imagery and signed up for the level two training. Helen Bonny herself was coming from the States to assist at the January residential training, and during that time my soul was challenged and nurtured in the deepest recesses. I felt connected at long last to the still, small voice inside. When the trainers stood in the final circle with us as that part of the training came to an end, I looked directly at one of the trainers and said, maybe to myself or maybe out loud, "I want what you've got!"

This was the year that I got to experience for myself, in all its intensity, that the heights and the depths are one. Looking Inside had brought to life a photo I had seen in a reflection book back in the early seventies of a small, yellow flower pushing up through the snow. The accompanying quote from Albert Camus was, "In the midst of winter I finally learned that there is within me an invincible summer."

It was time now for me to grow that little yellow flower into its fullest expression.

Jessica's Story

From New Mexico to Aotearoa, New Zealand, the southern hemisphere's land of enchantment. I arrived in December 1989 to start a new life. As we often do when setting forth into the unknown, I told myself that if it didn't work out, I could always leave. But I had heard the call, I'd Exited what passed as norm in the States, and I'd Looked deeply at the pros and cons. Now it was time to get on with it, as they say in Kiwiland.

I applied for permanent residency, with a lot of endorsement assistance from my new found friends and allies, fulfilling all of the arduous requirements for that process. I set about establishing the new counselling centre with my colleague. We were led to a lovely location where individual and group sessions could happen easily and smoothly. We began putting out the word, and soon the centre was humming with productive activity. We created a beautiful, nurturing ambience with lots of colour; it was a bit quirky but had solid professionalism. It was a success, and we were both gratified with the results.

By day I got on with the affairs of the centre. By night I trembled. I found that many nights I woke around 3:00 a.m. with huge fears. I tossed and turned and did my best to calm myself, but frequently I was awake the rest of the night. One night I remembered Louise Hay, particularly a healing tape she'd made early on to complement her book *You Can Heal Your Life*. I set up the recorder by my head and began the tape. I was asleep in no time, lulled and calmed by her soothing voice. Night after night, I

se."
of
go

pressed the button, and soon was deep
again. My gratitude knew no bounds.

;

ole sleeping mat was on the floor, with my
ny head and my torch by my side. One night I
ual and turned on the torch. Out of the corner
, I noticed something moving towards me, some
away on the floor. I shone the torch on it, and
as the biggest weta one could imagine. For those
not familiar, it is a big, black, beetle-like creature
seemingly huge legs and antennae. For some of us,
a fearsome sight. For me that night, it personified all
y fears. I was able to find a drinking glass and cover
he monster, removing it in the morning, but, oh, was I
grateful for Louise that night!

It turned out the fears were mostly about, "Can I make it here, alone?" I had education, I had developed skills, I had a likeable personality. I had enough chutzpah to make things happen, and I had a lot of experience. Logically, what was there to worry about? But that matrilineage patterning of dependency on a man to protect and provide was really strong. I like to think that my efforts to confront and dispel that pattern alongside countless other brave women doing the same have substantially contributed to the new freedom we now see most everywhere in the Western world. There's a fresh, prevailing wind that says woke with fears, pressed the button, and soon was deep in slumberland again. My gratitude knew no bounds.

My comfortable sleeping mat was on the floor, with my recorder at my head and my torch by my side. One night I woke as usual and turned on the torch. Out of the corner of my eye, I noticed something moving towards me, some distance away on the floor. I shone the torch on it, and there was the biggest weta one could imagine. For those of you not familiar, it is a big, black, beetle-like creature with seemingly huge legs and antennae. For some of us, it's a fearsome sight. For me that night, it personified all my fears. I was able to find a drinking glass and cover the monster, removing it in the morning, but, oh, was I grateful for Louise that night!

It turned out the fears were mostly about, "Can I make it here, alone?" I had education, I had developed skills, I had a likeable personality. I had enough chutzpah to make things happen, and I had a lot of experience. Logically, what was there to worry about? But that matrilineage patterning of dependency on a man to protect and provide was really strong. I like to think that my efforts to confront and dispel that pattern alongside countless other brave women doing the same have substantially contributed to the new freedom we now see most everywhere in the Western world. There's a fresh, prevailing wind that says to younger women, "You can do anything you choose." But it wasn't always so, and it still isn't in many parts of the world. So relish that freedom, young women, and go for it in the best ways that you can.

As my fears gradually lessened and my confidence grew, I spent more time alone in the spectacular beauty of New Zealand's nature. One warm and sunny day, I was lying on the nurturing sand with waves gently lapping nearby. No one was around, as is often the case at these precious beaches. That Twilight Zone, dozy, half-consciousness was upon me. I began to feel myself gently spiralling down, slowly swirling towards what I felt was the centre of the earth. There, a huge pool of ultraviolet invited me to immerse myself. I floated in this bath of ultraviolet energy, totally held and totally loved. Eventually I felt myself rising on the same spiralling energy towards my body lying on the sand. I became aware of myself lying on a condensed cushion of the ultraviolet energy like a placenta, connected through the spiralling cord to the great womb of Mother Earth. I was and am being fed, nurtured, and revitalized through that cord from the centre of the mother. I have come to think of it as the heart/womb centre of the mother. You are invited to feel your own placenta and cord connecting you to the heart/

womb of the mother, holding and sustaining you, loving you always, feeding you with vital life energy.

I share this visualization, this knowing with you because it is my pearl of great price from that solo period. I held it close for a long while, but she has asked me to share it with you now so that you may also feel this incredible, nourishing love with which she sustains us. We as women have a keen appreciation of Mother Earth, through our resonance with her moon and the seasonal cycles. Communing with her is one of the best ways to open spiritually. She can be your guide through a solo/solitude time. She awaits you … Inside.

Chapter 4

eXamine: "Wake Up!"

The Synchronicity Mirror

In daily life or during a structured quest, it is wise to cultivate attention to synchronicities. A synchronicity is more than a meaningful coincidence; it is an encoding of a message for you personally. You, and only you, happened to be in exactly that place at exactly that time to see and fully appreciate that message. Whether it's a song that happens to come on at that moment, a license plate on the car in front of you, a sign on a billboard, an article in a magazine, or a mention of a word that you've heard twice before that day, the messages can come in many hilarious and serendipitous ways.

How many of them do we miss by not staying awake to the possibilities every day? They are part of the intelligence of the universe, and believe it or not, it has you in mind. Yes, you! Each one of us is essentially important to the intelligence. We each have a key part to play in the universal drama. Yes, it's true: we are grains of sand amongst the trillion other grains. Being present with this ultimate paradox keeps us both humble and completely confident. We have grown as a species to where we are now able to hold the both/and. We can know that we are specks in the vastness, and we are precious beyond measure to the Greater Than.

Mother Earth is gently trying to get your attention every day with her winks and nods, her signs that seem to magically appear. Sometimes they are so overt and obvious that they're impossible to miss. Often they are more subtle, and one could easily laugh them off. Here is a plea: don't shrug and dismiss. You could be missing the most fun you've ever had!

There may be a cost to paying attention to the signs and synchronicities. You just might be called to change a bit here and there—perhaps even a big bit. Our long experience and observation is that it's worth it. What happens as a result of paying attention to the nudges and the messages is that your life becomes more fascinating and rewarding. Doors open that you couldn't have imagined possible, and you live in the flow. Because you have been awake, you have listened, eXamined, and you have acted.

As they say, if you don't like the mirror, change it! The mirror is the combination of external circumstances in your life, staring you in the face. Are you happy with the place you are living? Does it make you sing when you walk through the door, or do you at least go "Ahh" with a nice, warm feeling in your belly? If not, could it be time to change the mirror? Are you happy with the ways you are offering your wonderful gifts and talents to the world? Is there a nice, balanced exchange (financially or otherwise) for what you are offering? If not, could it be time to consider other options, perhaps even something you have loved but never thought you were good enough to make it your main focus?

And how about the special people in your life, your best friends, your significant other? Do they fill your world with delight, respect, and compassionate understanding? Are they truly there for you, as you are there for them? If not, could it be time for some gentle releasing and calling in the new? Please, no "chop-chop" here. People's hearts are involved. However, staying true to yourself and eXamining the mirror can mean moving on. Do it in the same way you would want it done to you: with clarity, kindness, and conviction, remembering that moving on is a process, not an event. It takes time.

If the mirror is showing you things about your life that don't add up, or that obviously aren't for your highest good, hold on to the truth from the mirror. The world doesn't like a victim, and you won't get much mileage from hanging out in victimhood. As the Trekkies say, "Resistance is futile." It doesn't serve you. If you've **L**ooked in the mirror outside and **I**nside, e**X**amining the synchronicities, you will see and know the changes that need to be made. Hold this knowing close in your heart.

In quests or in life, especially in the solitude periods, it is best to watch the synchronicities and e**X**amine the mirror. It simply makes things easier, and it will draw you closer to your spiritual self, who is actually the one in charge. In fact, we are spiritual beings having a human adventure. The more we acknowledge and run with that truth, the happier and more fulfilled we are.

Blessings on your magical e**X**amining.

Misha's Story

In 1994, I was finishing my thesis for my master's degee; preparing to cofacilitate our first quest together in Chaco Canyon and A-shi-sle pah in New Mexico and Hopi in Arizona; planning a six-month sabbatical housesit in Maui, Hawai'i; and attending a family wedding in New

Jersey in January 1995. What an exciting life change! My responsible "be there for others and follow the norm" attitude was undergoing a significant shift. I had until November to do the final workings on my thesis, but Jess and I wanted to leave in May, so I handed it in on the night before we flew to Albuquerque to facilitate the quest journey for thirteen women. Some wonderful life-changing moments and experiences during that time culminated in a weekend of witnessing the hypnotic dances at the Hopi reservation in Arizona. It was such a privilege to be allowed to witness this ancient, powerful ritual that holds the world in balance, as the Hopi say.

Since getting together in December 1992, Jessica and I had put a lot of focus on eXamining the synchronicities of our lives and the mirroring we gave to each other as we wove our lives together. When we arrived in Maui in the second week of July, we fully expected a housesit to have become available. Our two elders, Beth Gawain and Romy Leah, had been looking out for a suitable housesit for us, but nothing was materializing. A friend contacted us from New Zealand and said that a psychic friend of ours could see us settled, but there was no roof on the dwelling. That sounded a little ominous, and then reality looked us in the face. What we came up with through Beth was that her daughter, Shakti, had a Bed and Breakfast on the north shore of Kauai, and below her place was Secret Beach, where we could camp if we chose to. We had our tent from our time questing in New Mexico, so we put our two main suitcases in storage in Maui and set off with our tents to Secret Beach. Hmm, settled and no roof! We had two two-person tents with us (when pitched, they stood waist high, so we could only sit up or lie down in them), very thin sleeping mats, minimum clothes, a few books, a couple of torches, and some degree of enthusiasm for the adventure. It was a challenge to let go of the housesit notion. All the extras and personal belongings to make our housesit comfortable were safely in storage, and we were stripped to the bare minimum. Fortunately for us, there was no restriction that year for length of time camping, because Kauai was still recovering from Hurricane Iniki (September 11, 1992), which had devastated the island and some people still needed to camp out. Usually there was a five-day permit required that was strictly adhered to, and one had to up sticks and move on within the required time.

We set up home on the beach, one tent for sleeping and the other tent for whatever. So began one of the most magical times of my life. Jessica cleared all around our tent space and made a lanai area for sitting out on. I had to work out how to get into the tent and leave the sand outside. I must add that the only camping I had done prior to this was in New Mexico during the quest in June, so there were daily challenges for me in adjusting to this life style. We had access to the beach by the three hundred or so steps down from Shakti's B & B;– coming down was a breeze, but going back up was a fitness challenge. No need for a gym membership here! Food was a challenge; again, we needed to strip away the norm and work out what we could safely keep on the beach. Neither of us were gourmet cooks at the best of times, so we set about eating celery, cucumber, and yoghurt and drinking water till we could work out some other way of managing. We did have a cooler, but no ice, so we could store some things in that. And what about my morning cup of tea? A week or two of minimal eating and drinking sounded fine, but we were to be here till December.

Not to worry—isn't that a lesson we learn over and over again? The managers of the B & B, Larry and Marilyn, were extra helpful to us, and we quickly worked out some reciprocal arrangements with them. In return for a space in the fridge on their lanai, the use of Goldie (Shakti's old car), and (luxury of luxuries) a warm, freshwater, outside shower, we helped with cleaning up at the place. There were also invitations from time to time to share an evening meal with them. How could we ever question our needs being met? Some other camper who had packed up and gone back to "civilization" left a tin kettle on the beach. We cleaned that up and re engaged our fire-lighting skills, and lo and behold, the mighty cup of tea ritual was once more established. Mind you, every so often we went in Goldie to the local bakery and treated ourselves to a good cup of coffee, as well as a bear claw or an almond croissant. We weren't exactly slumming it once we worked out a routine.

Life on the beach took on a natural rhythm: we went to bed when it got dark and got up at first light. The beach appeared to be clothing optional, and the people who came to the beach were there to relax and have fun. There were no amenities there except for a natural shower that came out of the cliff, so there were really only day comers and one other serious camper. Back then it was still pretty much Secret Beach. Early on in our stay, an older couple came almost daily to the beach attired simply in their birthday suits and carrying snorkelling gear. My introduction to them was straightforward and simple. She swam up to me and asked whether I was okay to connect, or whether I preferred to be left alone. That in itself endeared me to her—thoughtful and unintrusive. I happily agreed to connect, and she proceeded to tell me her name and added that she had had at least fifty lifetimes as a dolphin. This was a bit of a stretch for me at the time and involved gulping a mouthful of seawater as my jaw dropped open. She then introduced me to her husband, and so began an interesting and beautiful friendship. They were both retired and had moved to Princeville after Hurricane Iniki. They were generosity personified; we had several meals at their condo, and in the ensuing years they loaned us their Maui condo and car when they were in Prescott, Arizona. They also gave us use of their home and vehicle in Prescott on another occasion, which allowed me to visit the Grand Canyon.

However, the thing that stood out for me most, and that gives an insight into their generosity, was much simpler than what I have recounted. One afternoon when they were visiting us on the beach, she asked what food I missed most. I thought for about a second before I said, "Roasted potatoes!" We laughed together about our favourite foods, and then they were on their way. They had a long walk from third beach, where we were camped, to the public entrance to Secret Beach—a good half hour to get back to their car. Much later that afternoon, I saw them walking back towards us. They arrived with roast potatoes freshly baked and wrapped in tinfoil, with tea towels to keep them hot. What a gift! Although I invited them to stay and share them with us, they quietly refused and headed back to their car. Now that is thoughtfulness and kindness, and whether or not she had been a dolphin before, I was truly humbled by her thoughtfulness.

Another time we offered our spare tent to a guy who was setting up a tent near us. He had been digging in the heat, anchoring the tent, and flattening out the sand in front of it. He looked hot and tired, so I boiled the billy and called him over for a cuppa, which he gratefully accepted. The three of us got to talking, and it transpired that he and his wife had visitors coming from Japan who wanted to spend a night on the beach. He needed to put up another tent, so we offered him the use of our spare guest tent to save him all the hassle. So began another friendship. He would arrive on his outboard motorboat and swim in with watermelon for us on a number of occasions. Then one day he asked what I missed having while living on the beach. I laughed and said that I was tired of sitting up straight, and I missed having a chair to sit on and lean back on. Yes, you guessed it! A couple of days later, he came in his boat and swam to shore with a beach chair for me. He was so excited to bring it that he forgot to anchor his boat, and we both looked up at the same time to see his boat drifting out!

By October it was clear that we were going to run out of money well before December. We had our tickets and expenses all paid up to get to the East Coast for the wedding, but it was our day-to-day living purse that was decidedly meagre. We put our few remaining coins into creating a flier and offered a workshop on the beach. But how to advertise it? Well, trusty Goldie took us into the nearby town of Hanalei, where we looked around and came across Avana's Goddess Shop! In we walked, and the rest is history. Avana and her husband, Robie, were our angels in disguise. They had moved to Kauai in February that year and had opened Avana's. They worked twelve-hour days for seven days a week without a break. Not only did they display our flier and help us gather a small group of women to come to the workshop, but they offered me to work for them one day a week for sixty dollars.

What a buzz that turned out to be. Not only was I earning, but we were meeting new people and having fun running the shop. Robie and Avana were living in a bamboo grove. I kid you not. Robie was masterful. He created a kitchen and lounge area using pallets for the flooring, and he had sheets for drop-down curtains when it rained. They had a series of tents around the platform area and a guest tent in which we spent many happy times. Robie had even managed to jack up a shower with hot water! What a wonderful lifestyle, and what fun we had with them. They went away for a week at one stage, and they left us to run the shop for them. We made it our mission to boost their sales that week and give them a surprise. Jessica had a way with customers; they would wander in and be looking at the beautiful lava-lavas. Before one could blink an eye, Jess had women draped in the lava-lavas and learning all the different ways they could tie them. Then they needed matching jewellery, and of course they couldn't leave without gifts for the folks back home; especially the beautiful island-patterned bedspreads and cushion covers. I was kept busy at the till while Jess interacted with the customers and Enya sang happily in the background. We tried different types of music, but it was Enya who created the ambience for sales. Robie and Avana have become lifelong friends.

Yes, we had stripped ourselves down to the bare essentials and placed all our must-haves for the housesit in storage, but we were awash with generosity and kindness—riches that are beyond price. We simply had to say yes to the synchronicities that presented themselves and enter into the adventure. If you don't like the mirror, ask for change and follow the synchronicities. If you like the mirror being reflected in your life, celebrate. We surely did, and do!

Jessica's Story

I was settling nicely into my new life. The centre was humming, and we introduced a training course. The trainees were lovely, mature people, and one woman in particular was a delight, with effervescent spirit and energy. My days were full and fulfilled, yet I began to experience a subtle yearning. It had been nearly four years since I'd bid Richard the final farewell. I had had several lovers during that time, but I finally made a strong request to the universe: "Bring me who I need to relate to next, and show me just how closely I am to relate to him." To my utter astonishment, no one showed up. For a whole year, I had been celibate and truly on my own. In retrospect, it was a clearing of the decks.

But now the longing. I had a body-awareness session and realized that my left hand and arm were reaching out for another's. Paying attention to the sign, I took time to write out my specs for my next relationship, telling the universe, "I am ready." After putting it all aside, I went into a quiet though anticipatory waiting mode.

I was due to go overseas to help with a training there. My very good friend, the trainee, was driving me to the airport. When we hugged goodbye, I could feel a zoom of electricity through my body, but I paid no attention to it at the time. During an interval period at the training, I decided to take a long bath. While I was immersed in velvety water, it slowly dawned on me that my physical reaction to my lady friend was the same as I had had with men.

Unthinkable! Me, attracted to a woman? Not a chance. I had been with a man since I was fifteen, and here I was at fifty-one. I was a heterosexual woman, and that was that. But the sign was unmistakable. At that exact moment, my back went out, and I couldn't move. I tried turning to the left slightly and then the right. I felt excruciating pain. I knew I would never be able to get out of the tub. Crisis!

By some miracle, there was a pad of paper and a pen on the ledge at the back of the tub. I gingerly reached above, grabbed them, and began writing. I knew that my beloved cousin had had relationships with both men and women. The writing became an eleven-page letter to her, filled with all the unthinkables and what-ifs. Finally, I could allow myself to see that this woman fitted all the specs I had written. I had simply neglected to specify gender, never dreaming for a second there would be anything but a man showing up. Gradually the initial shock abated, and I could move again—no more pain.

As soon as possible, I called my friend, related my truth, and learned that my feelings were reciprocated entirely. We agreed to meditate on our awareness and see what spirit was saying. We independently came to the understanding that this was a soul calling through the heart that we would choose not to resist. We realized that the consequences of pursuing this relationship would be totally life-changing, starting with the fact that ethically we would both need to resign from the Auckland training.

And so it came to pass that Misha and Jessica moved in together. Misha resigned from the training immediately. But I, in my hubris, held on for quite a while, believing that somehow, some way, I could carry on because "they needed me." Big, big learning. Resistance is futile. "Let go sooner." The bottom line is that no one is indispensable to an organization. They may be pivotal, but there will always be another person, another way to carry on, as there was in this case. The training moved forward without me, and the trainees had exposure to teachers who were even more skilled than me. I was deeply saddened by the disruption to all of their lives, even though I knew there was somehow a rightness in it all.

Misha and I were exhausted with the to-ing and fro-ing of it all, so we decided to take a sabbatical. We would find a housesit in Hawai'i for six months and rest. We arrived on Kauai, another land of enchantment, and found that the only accommodation available to us was camping on a beach. We set up camp on Secret Beach, as arranged by our dear friend and mentor, Beth Gawain. Lo and behold, there was a resident pod of spinner dolphins! Once again, the dolphins had called me and us to their magic. Every morning we opened the flap of the tent to watch the show: biggies and littlies spinning outrageously up and out, shimmering in the sunny diamond waters. Sometimes we would plunge into the waters, surrounded by our playful friends, scanning us with their amazing sonar and whizzing all around us. Another pearl of great price!

By being alert to the signs, recognizing what was happening, and pulling up the courage to follow through with the letting go and moving on, I entered the next chapter of my life—one that would bring me some of the greatest joy and fulfilment in this lifetime. It pays to eXamine, Look in the mirror and wake up!

Chapter 5

Integrate: "Be Present"

The Seeing and Be Seen

You've had the courage to **E**xit the norm and **L**ook at all the pros and cons, weighing the options. You've **L**ooked deeply **I**nside and tamed some important dragons. You've e**X**amined the mirror of your life, watched the signs and synchronicities, and determined your course. What remains? You must **I**ntegrate. What does that mean, **I**ntegrate?

The Oxford Dictionary defines the word integrate as "to form a whole". And Integration: "The process by which a well balanced psyche becomes whole." So here we begin to have clarity about where the entire ELIXIR process is going. It's going toward wholeness and the re-membering of our parts, putting the parts together again in to a wholeness. Were they ever not together, or discombobulated, in the first place? Yes and No. Inherently we were, are, and always will be whole in the essence of our being. But personality absorbs all kinds of rubbishy, dismembering beliefs about itself along the developmental way that it fundamentally believes to be true. Like the "not good enough" message most of us have to some degree or other. Gradually, the ELIXIR process has shown us definitively that most of those beliefs need transforming, updating, so that we re-member who we truly are. And Integrate. Become whole.

What's the fastest, deepest, best way to Integrate all this change, all these parts? Tell your stories and be seen and received. We call this witnessing. We have found that there are two ways to anchor all the insights and clarities as you Exit, Look, go deeply Inside, and eXamine.

The first is witnessing to yourself. There is probably no better way to witness to yourself than to follow in the footsteps of the great visionary psychiatrist Carl Jung. What did he do when he, the leading pupil, had been dismissed by Freud (the acknowledged father of psychiatry), because of his insistence on the importance of the spiritual? He went away for two years on a life solo and drew. Did Carl Jung know how to draw? No more than you do. But he had the courage and wisdom to pick up the colours and express himself on paper. Lo and behold, the healing took place. As you can read in his biography, *Memories, Dreams, and Reflections,* he saw and learned things through his drawings that gradually brought him back to a state of health and wholeness.

You can too. From the moment you get the first glimmer or flicker of change coming, get out that drawing pad and some oil-based pastels. Let your hand choose a colour. Start moving your hand any which way with the pastel on the page. After a bit, let that colour be supported by another colour, then another. Keep going until you think you're finished. Pause and close your eyes. Take a couple of deep breaths. Open your eyes and feel what else needs to be added to the drawing. When it is finally and truly complete, sit back and let a title for the drawing come to you. Put the title and date on the drawing. Now put it away in your folder. Or better yet, pin it up on a wall or door where you will see it often. Don't let anyone else demean or even comment on your drawing. This is a precious representation of your inner truth at this time. Honour it, see it, with no judging.

Before picking up your pastel, you may like to invite your judge to go on a holiday. Each of us has a strong inner character that we like to call the judge. S/he has your best interests at heart, wanting to protect and keep you safe at all times. She is full of insistent statements, even commands, about what you should and shouldn't be doing at any given moment. S/he is useful and helpful in reminding you of the rules of life, like a conscience—but not when it comes to any creative pursuit, especially drawing. Politely direct your judge to the judges' conference on the other side of the world, where s/he will have a lot of fun and learn some fascinating new ways to keep you safe.

Before you hang up your drawing, do what is suggested in that great book *Drawing on the Right Side of the Brain,* Turn it upside down and sit with it for a moment or two. You will see entirely new things, and maybe they're even more clarifying than the "right way up." You may even want to give it a second title. You'll be amazed by the upside-down effect in many of your drawings.

Just remember that every drawing you do is loaded with messages for you. It is an "out picturing" or witnessing to your inner being and self at that moment. It is a diagnostic of where you are at and what's happening. As with dreams, you may not be able to get all the messages straight away. You may even feel that you could invite a trusted, uncritical friend or ally to have a look at the drawing with you, both right side up and upside down. What we have repeatedly seen over the years is that the very act of doing the drawing is healing and integrating. Allowing yourself to access messages and understandings from it is a bonus. No matter what you were told in school—and so many of us were told, "You can't draw, so let it go"—please override those early messages and just do it!

Drawing is perhaps the primo way of Integrating change. But our minds, full of ideas and words, need a format, and that would be journaling. Writing out your thoughts, stream of consciousness, and letting it flow out of you also has tremendous merit for Integrating, witnessing, and seeing yourself. You'll be astounded at the insights and learnings that come from journaling. As you probably know, any old bits of paper will do. Ideally, you will get yourself a lovely book that feels honouring of your own beauty. No matter how angry, frustrated, sad, depressed, or elated you may feel, it's all part of the magnificence of you, so write it out and let yourself witness the breadth and depth of your soul pouring onto the pages. You'll discover pearls along the way, and you'll Integrate the changes much faster and more easily and gracefully.

Speaking of grace, another right side of the brain way to witness to yourself is movement. Again, you may have been told that you are clumsy and are certainly not a dancer. But what we know is that every person has a dancer inside. It's our birthright to move with the rhythms of life. So choose some music—strong and bold, gentle and soothing, whatever takes your fancy at the moment—and let yourself start with a small movement such as a hand gesture or a foot tap. Just like with the colours, keep adding in till more and more of your body joins in, whether standing in one place or moving around the whole room. Feel the rhythms pulsing through your body, freeing and integrating all that is moving through you with the change. You'll love it! You may even have a few pearls of insight flashing through as you move.

At the same time, you might want to witness to yourself by making sounds. It could be growly sounds, or staccato chirps, or long and beautiful tones, or even a scream or two. No matter. Whatever comes out of your throat is the right sound for that moment. As with drawing, many of us were told, "You are not a singer. You cannot carry a tune," so we shut our mouths and throttle our voices. Now is the time to bust that old message, open the larynx, and let it out. Let it out, for goodness' sake! Again, you will find yourself freer and more integrated the more you witness to yourself in sound.

These are just a few suggestions of things we have found profoundly useful for self-reflection, the Integration that comes with truly seeing yourself. But what about being witnessed to? This is the second way to anchor all of the insights and understandings you have come to through your Exit, your Look, your Inside, and your eXamining. There is nothing more fundamentally healing and integrating than being truly seen by a silent, respectful, non-judging, present other. Sooner or later, in a structured quest or a big life change, there comes a time when it is critical to share your story and have it heard, received, and seen, as women of old have always done.

There is an incomparable freeing in this being witnessed to, especially a freeing from those old voices or tapes of "I'm not good enough." We all have internalized messages from early on, when our erroneous perception was that we had failed at this or that. We failed to help or save Mommy or Daddy, failed to have the right friends; failed to do well enough in school, failed to be pretty enough, and failed to be good enough. Whether these messages were outright spoken to us or we internalized them from assumptions, they were *never* the truth. A classic example is Mom going off for a slightly extended period to have a holiday or to tend to a health crisis in the family, and at age three you internalize this as, "I must be bad and not good enough, because Mom's left me." This sort of thing happens all the time. No matter how much love and acceptance we think we are giving our children, it's true that almost all children in Western society internalize some degree of "not good enough."

Right alongside the "not good enough" is that old nutter, shame. We build a smaller or larger morass of shame over the obvious (and also the seemingly inconsequential) happenings in our lives. Amongst the obvious are when there is no daddy present in the household, or no mommy; when Daddy or Mommy is drinking too much, and we have to keep the secret; having an affair that is either flaunted or surreptitious; when there's not enough money, and we don't have the "right" house, clothes, or food; when we move all the time; when we don't get picked in the line; when we are not pretty, smart, or good enough; or when people find out we have birthmarks or a bad habit.

The larger accumulation of seemingly smaller incidents in our early lives contribute to the morass called "I'm not good enough"—or even worse, "I am bad at my core." This is the bottom line of shame. Our experience is that it can only and finally be completely healed and transformed through the witnessing, the telling of the story or secret, and having it witnessed, seen, and received respectfully, lovingly, nonjudgmentally, and fully.

If the eyes are the windows of the soul—and they are—then having our deepest and darkest thoughts spoken aloud in our own voices, and letting ourselves be truly seen while speaking them, is deep healing.

As counsellors, we have had the privilege to witness transformation for many clients as they allow themselves to share the secrets, be seen, and be accepted fully and unconditionally. We know that one-to-one divulging and being witnessed to can be transformative. In our vast experience with groups, we have also seen that the power of witnessing is amplified by each woman present when it's a prepared and awake group.

There are important, even crucial parameters to be agreed upon in such a group setting. First, there is the clear, unmistakable agreement and commitment to confidentiality and anonymity within the group (i.e., "I can talk later about my experience without naming or talking about anyone else's"). Then there is the commitment to respectfully hold the silence while one of the sisters is speaking; to fully honour her time, voice, and story without comment and especially without judgement; to be fully present for her, listening intently and intentionally; and to receive her sharing with as much unconditional, positive regard as we are capable of, holding eye contact and turning to face each woman in turn as she becomes the one to share.

This is a women's circle at its best. Jean Shinoda Bolen has described the need for these in her book *The Millionth Circle*. We always include such circles in our questing, both in preparing for the solo and especially following the solo. You can create or find such a circle where you too can find the deep transformative healing of witnessing and being seen. There is much being made today of the notion that we must drop our stories and move on. Our experience is the opposite. We must be given the space and time to share our stories with trusted others. Only then are we freed from the burdens of carrying them alone. Only then can we let them spiral from the caterpillar angst of history in to the gracious butterfly of mystery. The mystery of who we are, including all the facts of our lives—sordid and exquisite, gross and evanescent, the magnificence, and the utter wonder of our spiritual beingness having this human journey, Integrating in our inherent wholeness.

In truth, the mystery in its greatest, vastest sense is all there is. A marvellous Indian guru, Naranisgatta, is attributed with saying, "In wisdom I know nothing. In Love, I know everything. Between these two my life flows." The deepest, truest wisdom is in the no thing, the nothingness of great mystery. Because the no thingness is love, and everything is held within it, in potential. Enter the great mystery of you; walk right in to it. Like the ultraviolet lake at the centre of the mother, find your way into the great mystery. There is the ultimate Integration, the most lovingness you have ever felt or dreamed of, the peace of mind and heart you crave.

Integration is many possibilities in many ways. Along with the Exit, the Looking, the Inside, and facing the eXamining comes the Integration.

May your butterfly emerge with brilliant, shimmering translucence.

Misha's Story

Integration is such a loaded word. What's being integrated, who's being integrated, how is it being integrated, and when does it happen? Does it imply that disintegration has to happen first? What disintegrates, and how?

As I reflect on my life to this point, I can locate several little and not-so-little disintegrations—letting go of fast-held religious beliefs when they were no longer relevant in my life, letting go of the stories of my childhood to allow their prior power over me to dissipate, and letting go of the stories in my life that told me I was less than. I had opportunities to tell these stories and have them witnessed both in counselling and with different groups of women at various points in my life. Synchronistically, with every disintegration there were gifts and blessings of Integration and reintegration—not without tears and angst, I might add. I didn't experience these moments as one plus one equals two. It was nothing as tidy as that, because they were not just events; they were processes. Many if not all of those processes were messy and not always exactly welcomed by me! Reflective hindsight is notorious for its twenty-twenty vision, but it gave me a way of noticing and many *aha* moments of recognition.

Remember the stories of Jessica and me on Secret Beach with the wonderful magic of letting go of stuff and living by the day? One of the fun memories was watching the spinner dolphins playing in the water in front of us. A number of times, visitors to the beach would head out on their surfboards to get close to them, but the dolphins would swim farther out. The closest in they would come if people were "chasing" them was in line with the lighthouse on the point—quite a distance out. I am not a strong swimmer by any stretch of the imagination, but one day I saw them in the distance, and no one else was around. I decided it would be fun to be in the same water with them. Out I swam for a while, and I luxuriated in the *idea* of swimming with dolphins. I focused on synchronizing my breathing with every third stroke as Jessica had taught me; I was definitely a head-out-of-water swimmer. In my reverie, I heard quite a noise, and

I stopped and looked around me. I was encircled by the pod, with some swimming under me. For a moment or two, I knew fear because they were so noisy, so big, and so close! Then I relaxed into the experience. I looked up and over and saw that I was way out, almost level with the lighthouse. I was in their territory. I stayed quiet and noticed how noisy they were—and how playful. I again remarked how big they were; they looked much smaller in photos in *National Geographic*! These remarkable creatures stayed in a circle around me as I headed back in to the shore; I was way too far out for comfort. After a certain distance in, they suddenly disappeared, but they had accompanied me to a safer distance from the shore. As all the good children's books say, "I arrived home tired but happy." Thanks to our delightful cetacean friends, who helped me Integrate the stuff-less simplicity of a sabbatical experience I would never have voluntarily chosen.

Alongside this experience of joy and play, as well as facing a fear and being guided, I was also processing on an inner, almost intangible level the death of my mother two years before, back in August 1992 after an eight-month intense journey with cancer. As per Mum's wishes, we had her body cremated and her ashes buried in Eden Gardens. The Catholic Church had always espoused burial; for those of us raised so fiercely with the images of souls burning for a finite time in purgatory or for eternity in the fires of hell, cremation was a bit of a challenge at that time. However, it was eminently sensible, so as a family we followed Mum's wishes.

One night on the beach early in November, when we were the only ones camping, I was awakened by this awful screaming. Yes, it was me, and I had screamed myself awake from a nightmare. In the dream, Mum was coming down three steps towards me, and I was running delightedly towards her. All of a sudden, she burst into flames and was reduced to a pile of ashes in front of me. It was a truly sobering moment of profound Integration at a very deep level. I had not done any outward processing of cremation as such, but the process was happening with and without my conscious awareness.

And so it has been in so many instances in my life. I can Integrate things consciously, and I can bury a process, but it will rise up to consciousness if I make time and space for it. I prefer not to have to wait for a nightmare— it's not good for the heart! Now I consciously attend to challenging and joyful moments as they arise wherever possible, so that I can make my process conscious and have it witnessed in right timing.

Jessica's Story

As the eldest of five children, I was naturally offered the role of Mommy's right-hand girl. It was a role I accepted early on and relished. I could listen to, support, and be there for my mother as much as she wanted. I often saw and heard things that were inappropriate for a child or young person. But it was gratifying to be told how good and wise I was, so I learned early on the skills of witnessing and being present for another in need.

As I entered my teens, the needs became greater and greater. Both parents were alcoholically spiralling out of control, so the listening took on hypervigilant watchfulness, anticipating the next drama or potential violence. At the same time, I became even more of a witness for friends in need.

It was something of a relief from the pressures of home and a demanding prep school to choose pregnancy and marriage in my late teens. I can remember sitting for hours holding and rocking that first baby, soothing him and me—probably my first semi-solo time in my life. I was on a life quest called motherhood, but I didn't create another opportunity until the children were grown to step into a full, awakened solo experience.

Dean and I were having a timeout, and I was seeing Richard quite regularly. The children had grown and had left home. I felt a new freedom such as I had never felt before. I signed up for a quest to take place in the wild Adirondack Mountains, on the East Coast of North America. Though I had been living for ten years in Indian country in New Mexico, I had little idea of what to expect from a quest. I didn't weigh the pros and cons; I simply knew I had to do it. In my bones, I undoubtedly knew I needed to weigh the pros and cons of staying in my "perfect" marriage.

Michael Brown was a wise and trustworthy guide and facilitator who had trained in the psychosynthesis techniques of Roberto Assagioli, following in the footsteps of Carl Jung. Michael asked us to pair up and take turns asking the other, "Who am I?" over and over again for at least five minutes. The questioner would write down the answers while the speaker went deeper and deeper with the answers. Though I had been meditating off and on for twenty years, reading all kinds of metaphysical and esoteric literature, and attending various spiritual courses and trainings, here in the wild of nature, being asked a question over and over again, I began to sense myself absolutely as a spiritual being having a human journey.

During the twenty-four-hour solo, I spent the sunny afternoon lying on my back near the lake. It was beautifully warm, so I took off all my clothes and baked in the delicious freedom of it all. Suddenly I felt a something landing on my belly. I carefully peered out of the corner of my eye and saw the most exquisite blue dragonfly. At that moment, there were several other tinglings as more landed. Mesmerized, I kept absolutely still, shocked and amazed and completely exhilarated at the same time. The dragonflies kept landing until pretty soon my entire body was covered with magnificent, shimmering dragonfly energy, faintly and gently humming. How could anyone be more ecstatically blessed? I filled and filled till I felt I was going to pop. Finally I had to move. They flew off in an azure cloud, and I lay there drinking in the never-to-be-forgotten kiss of the dragonflies. I felt, and feel to this day, that it was somehow the spiritual kiss of Integration from my soul.

After the solo, the group assembled in a grove surrounded by huge evergreens, and we processed the alone time. One after another, we were witnessed to with presence and respect as we told our stories. Never had I felt so seen and heard as in that group of relative strangers turned temporary sisters and brothers by the compassionate leadership of Michael. Structured questing became a part of my future during that experience, but I was not aware of it at the time.

While living in New Mexico with Dean, I had been exposed to much of the American Indian presence. The state is one-third Indian population, and there are pueblos or Indian villages up and down the Rio Grande River. We frequently visited the pueblos for Feast Day ceremonies, and I felt the natural inner calm of these peaceful people despite their subjugation and enforced occupation by Europeans.

But it was Robert Boissiere and the experiences with the Banana Clan that had delivered most of the teachings I now find invaluable. Robert had been adopted by a Hopi Indian family on Second Mesa in Arizona. There he had a vision of the Banana Clan, a way that his white-skinned apprentices could learn some of the Hopi customs and the profound Hopi Way. His Hopi family on Second Mesa thought his vision of the Banana Clan was hilarious for the play on words. The Hopi word for white person is Pahana, so we became the Pahana Bananas. In their ingenuous and open way, they treated us tenderly and respectfully, teaching us bits of their ways and customs by letting us participate in ceremonies.

Along the way, we built our own kiva on Robert's land north of Santa Fe, and we performed many a ceremony of our own in and around the kiva. Robert was a writer, teacher, philosopher, and mystic, but most of all he was a magician who was not entirely sexually balanced. I, who had received provocative sexual energies from my father in his drunken states, came under the spell of the magician and felt some yucky energies that I had experienced while growing up. Today I have gratitude for all that Robert gave me and us. At the time, I was spiritually confused by the mixed messages of great teachings and difficult energies.

I turned to another great teacher, Joseph Rael (or Beautiful Painted Arrow), a Ute Native American from south-west Colorado. He was leading a long dance at Ah-shi-sle-pah, near the great ruins of Chaco Canyon in New Mexico. Ah-shi-sle-pah is a strange and wild part of the Bisti Badlands, guarded by the Navaho sheep herders. Nothing grows in there, and the winds whip the sandstone into twisted, outlandish shapes—here an eagle, there a tortoise; here a wolf, there a bat. Creatures and crevices and hidden entries were everywhere, and it was an eerie, enchanting place that was perfect for a dramatic ceremony.

Joseph had us erect a number of poles in a huge circle on a particularly flat area that would be our safe container. He told us that we were to dance around inside that circle all night, till dawn. When we needed a break, we were to take over from the drummers and sit and drum for a while. We began as always in the American South-west ceremonies with prayers and cornmeal blessing. Cornmeal represents the Corn Mother, revered throughout the South-west as the great nurturer and sustainer of life.

It almost never rains in the desert lands of the American South-west. As we entered the long dance circle, the skies opened, and it downpoured. We moved around the circle in slow, rhythmic movements to the beat of the drum. We each went further and further in to our own worlds, into the great mystery. We felt neither cold nor wet, only the drums and our steps, which became increasingly slow as the soft sandstone squished into mud. The rains carried on, and the drum carried on, and our movements became even slower, each foot lifting a big glob of mud with each step. We were in another world of no thought, no feeling.

Shortly after midnight, Joseph called the long dance and led us into the warm sanctuary of the sweat lodge. We felt the bodily change in temperature, the cessation of movement, but we continued in our highly altered state to dream beyond dreams. Eventually we had the last prayer in the lodge, and we began our climb up the hill towards our tents on the ridge. Two steps up, slide back; three steps up, slide back. We laughed hysterically. What a way to come back into our bodies. We discovered the only way we could make headway up the hill was by gripping each other's hands and half dragging, half pulling each other slowly up the hill, all the while doubled over in hysterics. There are many paths to Integration, and humour is one of the very best. But the "dreamy" altered state can elicit profoundly Integrative revelations.

The next day, Joseph took us down into Chaco Canyon itself, into the biggest of the kiva ruins there, Casa Rinconada. It is no longer possible to go into that circle; we were blessed beyond measure. In the 1200s, the pueblo peoples had a thriving culture at Chaco. Tribes came from all directions to trade goods, stories, and information, and to share in the high ceremony. Archaeologists surmise that this was the great meeting place for peoples west of the Mississippi, which is a vast area. The energy at Chaco is palpable. One can feel the Anasazi, or Ancient Ones, everywhere.

Joseph directed us to tune into the four energies of Purity, Strength, Wisdom, and Love. As he softly chanted, we went into another world. First I saw a beautiful lady in white with stars round her head like a halo—Purity. I noticed that her left hand was resting on something. Slowly a lion appeared, magnificent in its huge stature, golden, completely composed, and contained within itself, in total attunement and obedience to the lady— Strength. Ever so gradually, one of the golden hairs on the head of the lion began to spiral upwards, and I drifted with it towards the sun. I entered the sun, surrendering to a deeply pleasant, floating goldenness where I was I, and other *I* s were there, but somehow we were all one. Yet occasionally we would meet another *I,* and as we floated through one another, we each experienced an ecstatic, orgasmic cascade of energy—Wisdom. I slowly became aware that I was drifting towards the centre of the sun. Now I was being pulled into the centre like a vortex as the goldenness gave way to less and less light, and I was drifting down, down, down into utter darkness, utter stillness, feeling completely peaceful. The last awareness before losing the I-ness—this utter dark, this utter still— is Love.

Eventually Joseph stopped chanting and talked us back into waking consciousness. I came back knowing this was the greatest vision of my life; it is my truth as much today as then, and always. Between the long dance and lodge and vision in Casa Rinconada, I felt more Integrated at deeper levels of myself than ever before.

I was grateful to the men. Grateful to Mose, the father of my two beautiful children who produced the four awesome grandies. Grateful to Dean, who expanded my horizons beyond my wildest dreams. Grateful to Robert, for leading me into the Indian dimension. Grateful to Joseph for opening me to my truth. And grateful to Richard, who led me to the softening.

When the dolphins had called and it was set that Richard and I would travel for six and a half months in New Zealand and Australia, for whatever reason we decided to lay over for a bit on the way home in Maui. It sounded like a good idea because I had never been there. Who hasn't heard about the lushness and beauty of Hawai'i? It definitely has a magical reputation. But I was wholly unprepared for my visceral response to Hawai'i. From the moment I stepped out of the plane, walked on the ground, smelled the fragrances, and saw the palms, hibiscus, plumerias, and bougainvillea nodding at me, I felt at home.

Growing up in the northern hemisphere, on mainland America, as an Aries, and the eldest of five siblings, I had at least four powerful forces training me in yang energy. I was super good at planning, organizing, and doing. I was list oriented and accomplishment focused. I drove too quickly and hurried through life on my left brain, in

Action Lady mode. Motherhood slowed me down a tad, especially solo mothering after my marriage with Mose came to completion. But I was studying for my bachelor's and master' degrees at the same time, so slow was relative.

When I remarried and moved with Dean from the East Coast to the desert land of New Mexico, the land itself, dry and hot and powerful, called me into chasms of depth. I had enormous inner experiences, and my spirituality was vastly expanded. But I didn't stop for long. Dean and I were the Go-Go King and Queen, travelling widely in the States and Europe, attending all kinds of stimulating psychological and spiritual conferences, and establishing two centres (one in town as a retail and networking outlet, the other in the suburbs as a workshop and retreat centre). We did our best to stay connected with our six children between us. Most of them were living in other states, but my little girl was becoming a teen and needed focus. Then there were all the classes, retreats, and workshops we ran at our centre. I began the postgraduate training in the Bonny Method of Guided Imagery and Music. To say life was full during the Dean years is an understatement.

When Richard and I arrived in Hawai'i after the six and a half months of moving around the whole of New Zealand and both sides of the Australian continent, we were more than ready to take it easy. There is something in the air in Hawai'i; they call it aloha. It's something like being put in a cradle and rocked gently with a soothing lullaby sung near your head. You have to give in. Everything calls you to a delicious laid-back-ness. You can feel the frazzles seeping out of your pores.

That first visit was an eye-opener, or more accurately a heart-opener. When my dear friend and mentor Beth Gawain moved to Maui, I took every opportunity to visit her there. Gradually I understood what Hawai'i truly meant to me. After all the men in my life, and all the yang "doing" energies, I had been led to the gracious yin land of New Zealand. I had been further led in to the arms of a female partner who is gracious, tolerant, patient, and cooperative, and who loves to play. I have never been known for any of those qualities, and I sorely needed them.

Misha and I knew that we had been drawn together by our souls; we knew that we were called to service together. Gradually we began to recognize that our mode of service was and is for the empowerment of women. In the 2000s, the priority is on the two of two together, as in working it out cooperatively together. This is a way of being that is natural for women. But for thousands of years, women have been severely suppressed and even treated as objects, to be owned and used as property.

Chapter 5   ELIXIR Women's Quest for Wholeness

In the female genetic make-up, there is an imprint of "less than." This must change—now. The urgency is for women to be so empowered that they can take their place beside men in all walks of life as equals and as partners in balance on this lovely planet. They can take their place with their full capacities for promoting cooperative and collaborative action, feeling confident in their voices and the articulation of their knowings. Facts, yes. But even more important, those deep-down knowings that can guide any proceedings toward diplomatic, conciliatory, collaborative results.

Misha and I also began to understand the pivotal concomitant in our spiritual expansion and therefore our mode of service. The parallel to the subjugation of women has been the eclipsing of the divine feminine. For thousands of years, many now believe, there was a long period—perhaps as long as 8 – 2000 BC—of matriarchal patterning that held a primary reverencing for the divine feminine. But with the rise and dominance of the patriarchal patterning in the last several millennia, that reverence has largely gone underground.

Now is the time when the honouring of the divine feminine in all her forms must return. Only through finding a balance of divinity in our collective psyche for the all-powerful divine male can we begin to Integrate the balance in our outer lives. We need the divine feminine like the air we breathe. Without her we are spiritually lopsided, and we will never be able to live harmoniously on Earth—never mind have the respect and rightful treatment for this body we live on called Mother Earth.

Misha and I have cultivated an awareness and relationship with the divine feminine, as more and more women are doing today. We weave her teachings, her ways, and her principles into all our own teachings and services. We feel that the empowerment of women must have an awareness of and a developing relationship with the divine feminine.

Every time we went to Hawai'i, we found our own attunement to her growing. Why? Because the land and the aloha spirit in the air promotes it. If you like, the goddess is alive and well in Hawai'i; she probably never went underground there. Softness, beauty, and yin seep into your bones. It's actually hard to push at anything; the pace is ambling. The people are mostly friendly and welcoming. You shed clothes and tensions and allow her to hold you on the warm sands, in the gentle rocking waves and in the balmy caressing breezes.

We began taking groups of women from New Zealand, Australia, and the US mainland to Hawai'i on quests. I would watch in awe as women's armour fell away, and they were held in the aloha softness and began to soften. They came back from their solos and were witnessed in trusting circle by caring and respectful others as we walked the great eleven circuit labyrinths, those archetypally feminine constructs of sacred geometry. We splashed and played together, singing and dancing, dressing occasionally in our goddess finery. We ceremonially released what no longer served us and called in the new way for our lives. I watched in awe as women went from their quests and transformed their lives, leaving behind outmoded jobs and sometimes relationships, and they embraced callings and avocations that had been begging for expression, sometimes for years.

In my awe, I felt the gentle, penetrating, softening and opening as never before. I felt the divine feminine in me not as an idea, but as a living and breathing reality. I felt completely congruent with myself, completely at home in myself, completely Integrated. Don't get me wrong: I still had my grumpy, grouchy moments or flare-ups, or residual issues of controlling. Like everyone else, I'm a work in process. But in the depths of my heart, Hawai'i, the quests there, and the aloha goddess brought me to a deep interior Integration that lives in me today. Blessed Be.

Chapter 6

The **R**eturn: "Live It Up"

To Live Your Truth and Vision

You have had the courage to respond to the call and **E**xit, which required a big fat **L**ook **I**nside. You skulked around and befriended those dragon fears. You e**X**amined the signs and sniffed out some amazing treasures, even a pearl of great price. You began the **I**ntegrating process, being witnessed to and affirmed by respectful, loving others.

Your ELIXIR adventure is almost complete—but not quite.

What remains? In our structured retreat quests, we always spend significant time suggesting possibilities for the **R**eturn. They say that the two most important things that happen to us are being born and dying. From a spiritual perspective, how we come in and how we go out set a tone for everything in between and beyond. The **E**xit, or going apart from the norm, and the **R**eturn to the norm are the two super thresholds. We don't mean to minimize any aspect of the journey; it's all vital and critical to your soul's growth.

The first step of preparation for the **R**eturn is getting crystal clear about the treasures. You will have written about them in your journal. Hopefully you will have drawn a mandala or two that helped to anchor the energies, visions, and experiences. You will have been deeply seen by the group as you talked about your gems. Now is the time to summarize in a line or two, "What happened? Who am I now? What do I absolutely know about myself now? Who have I become? What is my vision? How will I carry it forward?" Getting fundamentally present with the gifts of this precious time you have given yourself is an act of core self-respect.

Holding this clear awareness of what transpired, you are now asked to safeguard the treasure in your heart. Commit yourself to protecting it, to honouring it with every fibre of your being. That often means, "Don't talk about it!" The folks back home won't have a clue what you're on about. They like to see a few photos and hear how the weather was, listening to maybe one or two light stories. Mostly they'll just be happy you're back in one piece and available again to attend to them and their needs.

The caution admonition is to be very careful about whom you talk to and what you say. Remember that you can dribble the energy out of any big experience by prattling on about it, especially to people who aren't able or willing to be fully present with you—to witness in the fullest sense of the word. Sometimes even the nicest, most well-meaning people. You'll know who is able to be there for you. If you have any doubt, turn to the people who have shared the journey with you. They were there; they saw; they know. You can always call, text, or email them for support.

After the second step of committing to holding your treasures close in your heart, take the third step of committing to reaching out for support—you'll need it. You have done a huge thing. You are committed to honouring and living the new truths and understandings you have accessed. But part of you may slip back in to the norm and want to go back to how it's always been. Of course there was and is no Always. As the Buddhists keep telling us, there is only change. So in truth, there isn't such a thing as the norm. Our yearning for stability and status quo is so great that we will sometimes kid ourselves and try to "go to sleep" again. It's impossible. Once you awaken to who you really are, you can't forget. But sometimes you need support. You need help to be reminded as the "good" witch and the "bad" witch in the play *Wicked* agreed, "I have been changed for good."

If perchance you have been called to a solo retreat, quest, or time apart, hopefully you will have set up with at least one other person that you deeply trust to hold the energy for you and help you with a download or debrief upon your **R**eturn. Please know that your special time will be that much more special because you have valued it enough to share and anchor the treasures. For those of you who have been with a group, reach out to your fellow travellers to reminisce and to continuously remember what has touched you, moved you, and enlightened you.

You will have had an insight, a BFO, an image, a pearl that has awakened you more fully to what this lifetime is about. That pearl now resides in the chalice of your heart, but it must be taken out and held up to the light every so often. The shimmering translucence of immense beauty must be admired—the exquisite mirror of who you truly are. As you gaze upon this pearl—perhaps captured in your poem, your drawing, your writing—you will be filled again and again with the motivation and assurance that you can and you will live your truth, your calling, your vision, your mission in the world.

And what is this great vision? Sometimes it looks like a particular action that you are called to. It could be a relationship that must be pursued—or ended. It could be a health odyssey that you must take. It may be a particular project that is yours to set in motion. It could be a particular kind of healing, teaching, or creativity that is yours to develop. It may be a complete career change. Whatever it is, you have seen it, you have felt the nudge, and you know it is yours to do. Most likely it will involve some sort of service. And who's to place a value on small or large? Is tending the needs of another who desperately needs your help any less valuable than starting an international movement, or allowing yourself to paint again, a hobby you adored as a child but put away because you had to make money?

Our dear brother, Neale Donald Walsh, has recently been reminding us that the soul is not really concerned with your doingness. Your soul wants you to develop a particular quality in this lifetime, and it will use all of your doingness to bring you terrific opportunities to develop that quality. What about generosity, tolerance, kindness, or patience? Perhaps you've opened to the clarity of what quality you are developing. If not, perhaps you will choose to take some time apart—a structured quest, or however you design it—and muse with your soul on your quality for this lifetime.

Whatever your mission, calling, or vision is, committing yourself and dedicating yourself to it is the fourth step of preparation for the **R**eturn. You are crystal clear about what it is. You will protect it as you would any great treasure. You will get support for its care and actualization. And you commit to bringing it forth in your daily life one step at a time.

Therefore you **R**eturn. You face the little and big routines. As the wonderful Buddhists say, "Before enlightenment, you chop wood and carry water. After enlightenment, you chop wood and carry water." Nothing has changed, and everything has changed. Because you have prepared, you watch yourself choosing when and where and what to speak. In the everydayness, you discern the seemingly insignificant and often in-your-face signs for your next steps. You regularly take out your gem and remember what you are on about. You rededicate yourself and re-energize yourself for the living of your truth.

And so the quest, the time apart, comes to an ending, and the new phase begins. The little death and the little new birth, all in the same lifetime. Many are the doors that will close in one lifetime, only to lead you to the many doors that will open. In truth, everything is a cycle—beginnings, waxing, waning, completion, done, new beginnings—like the moon. Many indigenous people call her Grandmother. She surely teaches us about the constancy of change and the absolute surety of the tides of our lives. She teaches us about what is apparently our collective deepest fear: the fear of death. She shows us every month, every year, every decade, every century, and every millennium that there will always be new beginnings, and that the doorway we call death is actually an open door to a new adventure.

You say, "But how do we know it is true? Nobody ever came back." Well, that's what the story of Jesus was supposed to illustrate: there *is* ongoingness. But if you still need more, try the huge mass of Hindu and Buddhist literature referencing reincarnation and the life beyond. Read Neale Donald Walsh. Try listening to what we're saying. Try trusting.

Because this is the essential preparation for the big **R**eturn, the one we call death. Sooner or later, you will be preparing for this lifetime to come to completion. You'll say bye to this magnificent temple that has housed your spirit, your soul for this lifetime. Anyone over fifty begins to think about these things, even if it is just a glimmer. The longer you go on, the more opportunity you are giving yourself for a decent preparation. Bear in mind that the last breath can come anytime; one never knows. We are not supposed to know, so we'll live as though every day is our last. We'll live to the fullest and prepare for death, whatever age we are.

What is the big exit, the big **R**eturn, this creepy monster we call death? And how can we blitz into our crippling fear of it?

First and foremost, how about taking a good, hard look at your life. Be alone and quiet at home, or alone and quiet in a time apart, or alone and quiet on a solo in a structured quest. If you really get with yourself, you will own that almost without exception, you were doing the very best you could given the circumstances. Hallelujah! There may be a few mistakes you have made along the way. As Louise Hay says, if you learned from them, they're not mistakes. And besides, you've probably done more than enough by now to rectify and balance those actions.

Doing a review of your life is a majorly useful thing to do at any age. An easy time to choose is one of the decade markers: perhaps twenty, thirty, or forty but certainly fifty, sixty, and seventy. By eighty or ninety, hopefully you're well and truly reviewed, and ready. The idea with the review is to go through all of the events of each decade: the biggies, the challenges, and the blessings. Then ascertain what the gifts were from each decade that you have brought forward with you. Do that as thoroughly as possible for each decade. Ideally, you will do this in several sittings with a deeply trusted, witnessing ally; the whole process will be hugely cathartic and freeing. When you have all your decades completed, call a gathering of a few trustworthy, witnessing allies. Set aside at least three hours and tell your story, decade by decade—the story of your life. Allow yourself to feel it being received, accepted, and blessed by your circle of allies. You will find that this is one of the greatest things you could do to reconcile yourself with your life and how you've lived it. You will feel more energized and committed to thriving in the days remaining to you than ever, and your fear of the monster will evaporate.

Read all you can about death and the beyond, and do a life review. Third and most important, as they say in Alcoholics Anonymous, cultivate a conscious contact with your higher power, whatever you choose to call it. Talk to it. Listen to it. Become aware of it. Do so in any way that appeals to you. More and more, do it your way. Just do it! Along the way, you will find you are developing that quality called faith. It's beyond believing, beyond knowing, true and simple. It's really hard to drum up a fear of death when you have your higher power with you, in you, around you, and holding you. Somehow there's a big relief about letting go, trusting, and feeling deep down that everything's going to be okay.

Misha's Story

"I will not die an unlived life." That is the opening line of a poem Dawn Markova wrote the night her father died. It is also the title of the book that carries the poem. The full title is *I Will Not Die an Unlived Life: Reclaiming Passion and Purpose.*

My eye was drawn to the title of this book some years ago when I was in the States, and I had brought it with me to read when I was visiting Romy in Maui in 2009. I still haven't read it—I can't get past the title! The title has become a mantra for me and constantly challenges me to review each day of my life. As a young child in a Catholic school, we learned many Bible stories. As I have said in an earlier account, we were fed an early diet of the lives of the saints. However, the line from the Bible that reached into my young mind and tapped into my soul was, "I have come that they may have life and live it to the full." Synchronistically, both mantras came together when I was in Maui and reached right into my soul, challenging me. I had been on many quests throughout my life, some only within the confines of my inner search and others with groups to the beautiful South-west of New Mexico and Arizona, as well as the lush beauty of Maui and Kauai, and the dark beauty and magnificence of inner tube rafting in the underground caves of Waitomo in New Zealand. I have visited each of my chakras—the key template of our Mystery School— over and over again, and I have sought to release the stories and events that have caused blockages in my chakra system, which manifested throughout my middle adult life as dis-ease. I spent time claiming and reclaiming my history. On numerous occasions I did what Edward Morris said his main character did in his novel *Kathleen, Kathleen*: "The gate leading down the path to by-gone days edged slowly open and she stepped through." I stepped through that gate so many times—released the stories and brought forward the gifts of those stories all the while strengthening my chakras and energy centres. I had bucketloads of purposeful passion. I was creating my story, my mystery, bringing myself from history to mystery. I found the twelve circuit classical labyrinth of Chartres Cathedral a compelling way to walk to my centre, releasing what was no longer needed and calling in the gifts for the return. Jessica and I were so inspired by our first walk on the labyrinth in Grace Cathedral in January 1995 that we made it our mission to introduce as many people as possible to it. We were focused on supporting Lauren Artress from Grace Cathedral to realize her dream and vision of thousands of people walking the labyrinth on New Year's Eve 1999 as we stepped into the new millennium, calling in peace and harmony. We did so, bringing the portable labyrinth to our home retreat centre, Te Moata, on Paul Road just north of Tairua, New Zealand, for this very special walk.

However, I had another major challenge to manage: breast cancer—not once but twice. The first time was in 2002, and I faced it again in 2008. The first event in 2002 brought me to the knees of my soul as I stared the spectre of death in the face. I was being eyeballed, and it was far from comfortable. Yes, I witnessed my beloved Nana in 1979, a very close friend in 1991, and then my mother in 1992 through their cancer journeys. I had stood with them when death took them through the portal from this life to the next adventure. However, that was history, and I was now faced with my own mystery of life and death.

I was in very early stage of breast cancer in 2002, and I had age on my side, but something changed forever inside of me. I was leading as good a life as I knew how, and I was working passionately and purposefully—but that did not gain me what was called in my young Catholic life "indulgences". Some of you with a similar background of

Catholicism may remember doing the nine first Fridays every year, saying certain novenas over and over again in order to earn indulgences which were like an insurance plan for purgatory. The more indulgences you gathered into your spiritual bank account, the less time you would have to do in purgatory when you died.

I was traumatized by the diagnosis, and thought of cancer as a death sentence. For the first year the word "cancer" sat on the end of my nose and I was seeing life through that filter. By the second year when I joined the Breast Cancer Dragon Boat team, Busting withLife, "cancer" slipped into my peripheral vision With a lot of assistance from Jessica, my beloved mentors Romy and Beth, family, friends, and an online support group, I learned to walk into my centre and claim my life. I was living the **R**eturn from that centre experience, from the core of my soul. I was intentional about living fully and showing by example that life is lived one day at a time with focused consciousness, passion, and purpose.

In 2008 the cancer returned. It was only then, when I was faced with a double mastectomy, that I realized a bottom-line truth. Although I had quested many times and had faithfully lived the **R**eturn many times, I had ignored an aspect of the dream I'd had in 1989, the year I'd left my religious order. Remember the barren field with the crows pecking futilely at the soil, looking for sustenance? They were doing it with passion and purpose, because they faced certain starvation leading to death if they didn't. I suddenly saw a two-legged stool that kept falling over because the third leg was missing. Where had the leg gone, and who had taken it? Had I unwittingly cut it off? I followed the labyrinth path into my centre and waited there until the third leg appeared. Then I could do the **R**eturn journey.

What is that third leg? It is so simple, but it took me on a journey to my early childhood and my years growing up. I instinctively knew how to survive difficult and challenging situations, especially in boarding school for all those years. It was so simple and yet so profound: PLAY. Again my Catholic roots remembered a piece from the Bible. "Unless you become as little children, you will not enter the kingdom of heaven." Heaven is not some faraway place that you have to wait for and earn through indulgences. It is what we make of our very own here and now. Play is the balance for living with Passion and Purpose. It restores our sense of holding things lightly, and ensures that we remember fun and delight to offset the many responsibilities of an adult life

Our "umbrella" organisation, SoulPath Journeys, was born with the underlying philosophy that we need to balance our passion and our purpose with play. It is my time in my **R**eturn years to remind others by the way I behave. Live the soul's journey through this human expression in the balance of passion, purpose and play.

Jessica's Story

Enthusiasm. *En Theos*. In God.

Many times people have told me how they appreciated my enthusiasm. All my life, I have been about spirituality, both mine and everyone else's. It helps us to remember ever more fully who we are: spiritual beings having a human adventure. All my life, I have been enthusiastically spiritually guiding people, more and more consciously.

It's funny how in retrospect, one can see so clearly. Being there for my dear mama was my first preparation. Providing kitchen therapy for family and friends was the natural follow-on. Formalizing that avocation with a master's degree in mental health counselling took it forward professionally.

Working with Dean in the seventies came next, establishing our urban retail centre and distributing all manner of spiritual goods, as well as a rural workshop and retreat centre where spiritual teaching and healing were the focus. In the late eighties, working with my business partner and setting up the counselling centre in New Zealand with a clear spiritual component seemed like a piece of cake. It's easy to see how the outer, worldly steps of preparation were one, two, three.

Preparation for what? When Misha and I came together in the early nineties, all we knew for sure was that our souls had drawn us together. In the vernacular of our dear friend Shay, we defined ourselves as cardio sexual. I certainly couldn't call myself exclusively a lesbian, though it was helpful to know that the Kinsey Report concluded 80 per cent of all people were actually bisexual in nature, whether or not they acted on it. We were simply two women brought together in heart and soul. We were master's degree counsellors with lengthy intentional spiritual development. Surely the divine would lead us where we needed to go.

Misha had her background in the profound teachings of a religious order. I had the bountiful gifts from growing up in the folds of the Episcopal Anglican Church, with all its magnificent music and high ceremony. Then I had the exquisite gift of an older cousin who tutored me for years in all manner of esoteric and metaphysical wisdom. This was followed by an in-depth training from the American Indians, particularly regarding questing.

In the late eighties before I met Misha, another pivotal preparation had occurred. While attending a workshop in New Zealand, we were directed to a silent solo period in nature; we were to return with a symbol of our essence. I was drawn that day to the delicate beauty of the tree fern called the ponga and its spiralling koru shape. I drew the koru shape on paper, and suddenly the words sprung into the spiral: "I am a priestess of the goddess." These words augured hugely, though I had little understanding at the time.

Both Misha and I had had extensive preparation on the outer, and the parallel inner growth was just as key. It takes a lot of inner strength to leave a religious order after twenty-six years, where you've made lifetime vows. It takes strength to leave a marriage, never mind two, when you go into them with a lifetime commitment. It requires strength to leave the country of your origin, your children, your known world, and to trust that the new world will actually embrace you, never mind support your thriving. When you've walked through these mini deaths and mini rebirths, you come in to a knowing that no matter what, you'll get through, you'll be guided, and the Way will open.

Most important, there is purpose in it all. There's cosmic intelligence, or design if you like. There will always be a forward trajectory that's part of the plan. When Misha and I **R**eturned to New Zealand from our fantastical quest on Secret Beach, we did the obvious one step in front of the other. We carried on with our counselling work, and we carried on with the smaller workshops we had been doing.

But we had a pearl of great price. We had the vision of providing retreat quests for women in faraway exotic places they would not normally experience. We set up journeys first to the desert lands of New Mexico and Arizona, and then to the Hawaiian Islands of Kauai and Maui. They were popular and amazing. We saw time and again that lives were transformed. People **R**eturned from their quests and made huge changes, opening doors they never would have dreamed possible. Women stepped forward with new levels of empowerment and leadership.

Then one fine day, Misha **R**eturned from a visit to our eldress, Romy, with the birth of SoulPath. Oh, so that was what we'd been doing! Leading women on journeys, individually and in groups—both small journeys and huge ones—that aligned them with the paths of their souls. In the next instant, we found that we could have the domain name soulpathjourneys.com. Shortly thereafter, our beautiful accountant set up the legal entity SoulPath Journeys.

Shortly after my seventieth birthday celebrations in 2011, we had another birthing party: the formal launch of this new being called SoulPath Journeys. Our dear friend Camille Maurine, of Meditation Secrets for Women, gave the inspiring keynote speech. Our dear friend Mary Hunt did an evocative clairvoyant dance. And our dear friend and personal assistant Sally Mac delighted everyone with her inimitable Fairy Heartstar granting of wishes. Many of our dear friends coordinated a scrumptious supper. The new being was deeply honoured and welcomed to the world.

That new being is now five years old. She has grown quietly and steadily in a sweet-natured way. She has gathered a circle of wise women aunties who watch over her. Metaphorically, in the New Zealand educational system she is going to school because she has turned five. She is coming out into the world. Perhaps this very book is part of her emergence into a wider context, along with her updated, snazzy website.

What will she become? How does any mother know what her child will become? All we know is that we will continue to nurture and mother her as the child, the outer expression of our mission together in this lifetime. As for the women who come to our courses, whose lives are uniquely precious to us—we will cherish them all, even as we each attend to our own inner mission of soul growth.

My mission on the **R**eturn is to draw ever nearer to my goddess, my soul. I am happy to say she and I have developed quite a dialogue. She seems to be infinitely patient with my Aries impatience. Yet I find her nudging me along with instant knowings on a day-to-day basis. I wish that I were 100 per cent conscious of her presence. I am not, but I am working on it. I am completely filled with gratitude for her grace and glory, and sometimes I feel an absolute oneness with her. Nearly all the time, I feel an alignment and attunement with her, and I'm following her path. Thy will be done.

May your quest **R**eturns be safe, smooth, and one-der-ful!

ELIXIR: Conclusion

Exit, Look Inside, eXamine, Integrate, Return. This is the ELIXIR of wholeness, the women's way, the life's journey.

As we said, all of life is a journey, a quest, from the Great Before to the Great After. We have all Exited the norm in the Great Before and chosen to come into this lifetime because it is a privilege to come to the Earth School of Free Will. We have all Looked over our options, decided what we wanted to accomplish in this life, developed a mission or intention, and chosen the country, the skin colour, the sex, the parents, and the genetic make-up that would best support our intentions. We have all chosen or been pushed by circumstances into solo, Inside times where we could confront fears, see things more clearly, and access pearls of great price. We gradually learn to pay more attention to the signs and symbols along the way, to eXamine the mirror of our external lives, and to use synchronistic *aha*s as a trustworthy navigational GPS. We work on Integrating the varied experiences in our lives in many ways, making excellent headway when we allow ourselves and our sharings to be witnessed by caring, respectful others. And we will **R**eturn, sooner or later in divine timing, to the Great After, hopefully having made considerable headway on our soul mission and intention, bringing some pearls of great price with which we may continue our service there, until the next **E**xit call comes.

In this quest called life, or a lifetime in Earth School, the main thing we do is choose. Every day and all the time, we choose what we will think, say, or do. We who have chosen the female gender are in unique situations of choice, because it is our time. This is the millennium when the female values of relatedness, cooperation, and working together for the good of the whole will prevail. We can choose to walk our talk in an empowered, congruent way that promotes and models these values— or not. We can continue hiding and cowering in "less than" corners—or not. What will each of us choose, and why?

The planet, Mother Gaia, needs us to choose wisely. The patriarchal times are waning and have brought us to the brink of extinction, alongside so many species. If we don't stand up and be counted, if we don't make our voices heard, if we don't step up to the requirements of change now …

So what can you do? How are you tending your chalice of wholeness for yourself, first and foremost? With what kind of beautiful and inspiring material are you feeding your mind each day? With what gentle nurture are you tending your heart and emotions each day? With what stretching activity are you extending your physical body each day? Most important, with what form of communion are you dancing with your spirit each day?

This daily balance of attention to our illustrious four-body system is the way to create and fill your chalice with the elixir of wholeness. In the big quest called this lifetime, we are each responsible for creating a container, a vessel, a chalice if you will, in to which we can pour the elixir of daily wholeness attention. You can call your chalice your body, if you like, or your whole energetic being. You can hold an image, draw a mandala of it, or make a clay representation of it. It's your creation, your chalice. What you fill it with is your choice. What we hope, trust, and exhort you to fill it with is the nectar of wholeness—all the goodness, truth, and beauty that aligns you, your personality self, with the greatness of your soul and its path of evolution.

Yes, each soul has a path and a destiny. Its development on that path has everything to do with the choices you make. Your soul needs you to be as whole, healthy, and holy as possible. Your soul needs you to be as aligned, congruent, and cooperative with it as possible. Your soul must grow itself through you. Your soul wants to come fully in to you so it can shine its radiance through you and contribute to the awakening of the species called humanity.

You, walking in balance and wholeness, passionately, purposefully, and playfully aligned with the path of your soul, are an empowered woman, standing equal with any man and making a difference to Gaia and humanity.

This is the call. This is the women's quest. This is the ELIXIR of wholeness.

Printed in the United States
By Bookmasters